W9-DFK-142

HOW TO GAMBLE AND WIN

EDWIN SILBERSTANG

CORNERSTONE LIBRARY

Copyright © 1979 by Edwin Silberstang

All rights reserved, including the right of reproduction,
in whole or in part, in any form

Published by Cornerstone Library
A Simon & Schuster Subsidiary of
Gulf & Western Corporation
Simon & Schuster Building
1230 Avenue of the Americas
New York, New York 10020

This new Cornerstone Library edition is published by arrangement with
Franklin Watts and is a complete and unabridged reprint of the original
hardcover edition

The trademark of Cornerstone Library, Inc. consists of the words "Cornerstone
Library" and the portrayal of a cube and is registered in the United States Patent
Office

Manufactured in the United States of America

ISBN 346-12451-4

To Roy and Louise Friedman

CONTENTS

ALL ABOUT GAMBLING

I. GAMBLING—A DEFINITION

Before discussing the subject of gambling, I believe that a good working definition of gambling should be stated. This will not be the abstract dictionary definition but one that has been made realistically from actual play and observation of the gambling world.

Two key words in the definition are "luck" and "chance." The words will be used synonymously and will be defined as "an unpredictable and unwilling element in any occurrence; one over which the player has no control."

The three-part definition of gambling is as follows:

• It is the risking of money on the outcome of any game of chance or other activity, such as a sporting event or horse race, over which the bettor has no active control.

The first part of this definition covers games such as craps, roulette, baccarat, keno, slot machines, horse and greyhound races, and any other games played with any kind of apparatus in which the operator has partial or full control of the equipment.

- It is an activity in which the casino, bookmaker, racetrack, or other operator has an advantage over the player, who hopes to overcome that advantage by luck.

Every casino game, with the exception of blackjack, has a built-in advantage or edge for the house. This advantage may run from 0.6 percent all the way past 50 percent. Every bet made with a sports parlor or bookmaker carries a disadvantage to the bettor called "vigorish," or "vig," of from 4 percent to 10 percent. The average racetrack take or edge on the total handle is between 18 percent and 20 percent.

- It is the involvement in any card or other game where there is a combination of skill and luck involved and where, although the skillful player will win in the long run, the unskilled player, in a short series, may overcome that skill by luck or chance. Or it may be betting on one's skill in a game like golf or billiards, where the more skilled player will give away points or strokes to make the game one whose outcome is in doubt.

In certain games, such as gin rummy, poker and backgammon, a combination of skill and luck is involved. In the long run, the expectation is that the more skilled player will win; but in a short series anything can happen because of the element of chance, and a less skillful player may come out ahead temporarily.

When poker is played in a casino, the house takes a cut from every pot, which in theory immediately puts all the participants at a disadvantage; although skill can overcome that advantage if the house cut is not too great.

When poker is played in a card club, the operators collect rental fees by the half hour or hour, again placing the players theoretically at a very slight disadvantage.

Only blackjack, among the casino games, when played with optimum rules, gives the player the advantage at times over the house; and this game will be discussed at full length in the chapter on blackjack.

This definition counteracts the careless ways by which gambling is usually defined. Many people say or think: "Life is a gamble. Everything is a gamble. When we wake up in the morning, or cross the street, or open a business, or do anything, it's a gamble."

But, according to the foregoing definition, "life" is not a gamble. You don't risk money on events over which you have no control when you get out of bed in the morning, or cross the street, or go to work. Even when you do risk money by going into a business or buying land, you aren't gambling, because the outcome is not completely out of your control; and businesses and land purchases are not usually rigged by operators who, in selling them, maintain an advantage over the purchasers.

At times, there may be a fine line drawn between investments and gambling. For example, a farmer might buy commodities in a crop that he grows, such as wheat or corn, in order to hedge against crop failure or falling prices. That's an investment. Another person might buy enormous amounts of wheat or corn futures on margin, using the margin as leverage for possible huge gains or losses. That's gambling.

For the short term, people putting money into the stock market or commodities exchange have little control over the outcome. World events or weather vagaries might upset the market tremendously and cause a break in prices which will wipe out those who used margin for leverage. Investors, however, have control. They can ride out the short swings and hold onto their stock or commodities. Just because investors may end up losing money doesn't mean they are gambling.

The more control one has and the less the outcome is in the hands of chance, the less it is gambling. Conversely, when most of the results are left to chance or luck, the result is a gamble. Whether one loses or wins as a result of this, doesn't change the definition.

If losses were the only criterion, then people who put their money into savings accounts, where inflation robs the interest payments of any purchasing power, would be said to be gambling. But we know that isn't the case. A bad investment, per se, is not a gamble.

Another fallacy that is widely believed is that the more you know of a subject, the less likely for it to be a gamble. No matter how many figures or facts you know, no matter what your knowledge of conditions, if the outcome is left completely to chance—it's a gamble.

This is particularly true of people who bet on horse races. They feel they are "investing" and not really gambling. After all, they've made a study of track conditions, speed ratings, past performances, weights, jockeys, distances, and on and on. They are full of facts and full of figures, which they can quote to you for hours on end.

However, the tapped-out horseplayer at the end of the racing day is a sad cliché. He sits and wonders what went wrong. The horse in the fifth race should have won, and the horse in the eighth race was a sure thing; yet both finished far down the track. The next day he is back with his *Racing Form,* studying the figures all over again, with the same dismal results.

Betting on horse racing is gambling because there's not enough information in all the past performance charts and racing forms to overcome chance. There are too many variables that can never be seen or understood. A horse can't talk and can never really reveal its true condition on the day it races. The jockey might have had a bad night, and the trainer might have instructed the jockey to take it easy that day. This information will never be revealed to the bettor.

And even if average bettors had sufficient information about one horse, there are other horses entered in the same race that are a mystery to them. They can't speak to all the jockeys and trainers and personally know the condition of every horse in a race they are betting on. To top it all off, the track takes 20 percent of each bet, and horse race bettors are working from a frightful disadvantage, making it practically impossible to "beat the races."

Thus, whether you make money, or have an enormous number of facts at your disposal, or feel you are not really gambling makes no difference whatsoever. If you don't have control and if luck or chance plays a major role, no matter what you call your involvement, it is gambling if money and risk are involved. This is not to say that gambling is synonymous with losing for this book will show you how to gamble and *win,* with an intelligent and selective approach to certain gambling games and situations.

II. WHY WE GAMBLE

There are many changes in official morality sweeping the United States today, and one of the most important involves gambling. More and more states and communities are legalizing some form of wagering; and as the years go by, gambling will probably be as routine and legal as the sale of liquor is today.

The reasons for this are twofold. First, states and cities around the country realize that enormous revenues can be garnered from legalizing what most people are doing anyway. More importantly, *people want to gamble*; they like to gamble and nothing, not even laws forbidding them, will stop them from gambling.

The average person finds gambling to be fun and exciting, a pastime for amusement; yet, unlike a great many other pastimes, there is a serious problem involved if it is overdone. For, in order to gamble, something must be at stake; and what is at stake is money, generally hard-earned money, money that can't easily be lost without pain or some unpleasant consequences. But many people dismiss their predilection to gamble excessively with the observation that "life is a gamble anyway, so why shouldn't I make all the bets I want to?"

Is this really so? Is life a gamble, and is this the reason so many people are not only willing but eager to gamble? By our definition of gambling, life is not a gamble at all. If life were a gamble, then there wouldn't be any organized gambling as we know it now, because the uncertain aspects of life would contain enough excitement and thrills so that a horse race or craps or poker game would be dull stuff in comparison.

But the harsh truth is that life not only isn't a gamble but holds few uncertainties for most of us. Life, for the vast majority of people, is quite predictable. We have jobs or vocations that we devote most of the day to, and then we plan short vacations at the same time each year. We get married and have children, watch them grow up, and save for their college education. We worry about the future and thus we plan how to negate the dangers of old age and its insecurity. In other words, the thought of uncertainty in our lives creates enormous anxiety. We plan carefully to avoid any uncertainty. We show up at work in the morning and go home sometime during the evening. We take care of our families or our business. Little is left to chance. We want security at all costs and we plan carefully to ensure this security.

However, the world of gambling is just the opposite of our ordered, secure world. When we gamble, we don't know what is going to happen next; we cannot predict the future. We have little or no control over the outcome of what we are betting on. We are, in short, in a world fraught with uncertainty. And yet it is this uncertainty that causes a vivid moment of suspension of knowledge, when all is left to chance: that is the exciting part of gambling for most people.

One of the chief lures of gambling is to test the unknown, and it is most easily seen in the dynamics of slot machines, which are everywhere in casinos and which yield the casinos an enormous income. Women from lower income brackets generally play the slots, for they know the value of the dollar in the household and feel less guilt when they risk a few dollars worth of nickels to "try their luck." These same women would be loath to bet several dollars at a time on a game like blackjack or craps, but they feel at home at the slots. Casinos that make most of their income from slot machines know this and cater to women, offering side prizes of nylons and cosmetics.

Each pull of the machine causes these women to enter that unknown world at a slight risk. What will happen next? Will the next pull be another loss or will the jackpot hit this time?

If casinos combine this fascination with the possibility of a large payoff, they attract men from the same lower economic brackets to the slots. That is the reason for the recent proliferation of dollar slots and progressive machines. Now another element has been added to the lure of the uncertain result, and that is the possibility of a huge payoff. Some progressive slots pay off in the hundreds of thousands of dollars for a few dollars' worth of play.

When you see people playing the big progressive machines, their fascination is apparent to any onlooker, and the fascination is contagious. What is going to happen with the next pull? There is no way to really know until the money is inserted to make the machine operative. It can come up empty or a red light might go off, bells might start ringing, and $100,000 might be paid out.

A gambler can spend hours in front of the machine feeding it dollars and still feel the same thrill every time the handle is pulled. This might be the lucky one! And once hooked, it is hard to get away, for suppose, horror of horrors, that after leaving, the next player hits that tremendous jackpot. That sort of gambler's calamity might haunt the player for years to come with the thoughts, "If only I had stayed for that one extra play. If only I hadn't been so impatient." The player thinks this after spending five hours at the machine!

The casino operator is fully aware of this fascination and takes advantage of this knowledge to set the machine for a very lucrative income for himself. He knows just how patient the woman playing the machines is, waiting and hoping for that giant payoff. She may be the same woman who earlier that morning screamed at her children at the breakfast table for dawdling over their food and harangued her husband for being five minutes late. But at the slots, that is a different story altogether. This is not humdrum and dull life; this is something else. To put it in a nutshell, this is gambling.

Any gamble that combines the uncertainty of outcome with the chance to win a lot of money for a small investment becomes enormously popular. Casino games such as the progressive slots and keno, where a 70¢ bet may net $25,000, are matched by state lotteries and private illegal ones, where bets as low as a dime may reap big payoffs.

It doesn't matter how bad the odds are and how slim the chances of winning. The important thing is that there is a *chance*. Someone has to win a lottery, and it could be me, thinks the person purchasing a ticket. The lure is tremendous, even though lotteries may place the ticket buyer at a disadvantage that is almost impossible to overcome. Illegal lotteries, which pay off at 500–1 or 600–1, give the operator a 50 percent advantage. And state lotteries, which siphon off a great deal of the money bet, can be just as bad; but it doesn't really matter to the ticket buyers. They might still win. Anything is possible.

So people will continue to play the lotteries and the slots and keno, for how else will they be able to make so much money in so short a period of time? Certainly not in their ordinary way of life. When you work for a living, the possibility of a giant payoff as a reward for good work is practically nil.

This same principle has been recognized recently by racetrack owners, who, in an effort to increase revenues, have introduced exotic betting schemes at the races. Triples, exactas, superfectas, and quinellas are now standard features at tracks that never had anything more fancy than the daily double. Bettors who normally wagered money on straight bets now put their money on these seductive bets in an effort to win a small fortune at the track without investing more than $2 or $5.

It's the same principle in operation—a big payoff for a small bet, with the outcome uncertain and dependent wholly on chance and luck.

While women are attracted to casino games such as slot machines and keno, men have long been involved with the table games, such as blackjack and craps. Those from the lower economic strata play in the smaller games, with minimum bets of $1 and $2. The more affluent play in the bigger games, but the games are basically the same, no matter what the minimum bet.

The bettors at the dice or blackjack table are there for the same excitement that holds the women at the slot machines. But in these games, there is no big payoff available for a small bet. To win big you must bet big. In order to win a lot of money, you must risk losing a lot of money. Which brings us to the next reason for gambling, and that is the *thrill of anxiety.*

To get this thrill, gamblers purposely create their own tension. They put themselves into risk situations where the outcome, as in all gambling games, is uncertain and may cost them money. The greater the risk of loss, the greater the loss would hurt them, the more they are thrilled. In this kind of anxious state, the suspended moments when the outcome is uncertain become painfully exciting.

A man betting beyond his means, with a $1,000 bet on the line in craps, can certainly feel his heart beat fast as the dice are thrown. Lady Luck will either favor or hurt him. He has no control whatsoever over the plastic cubes thrown across the table. But this anxiety is thrilling; an artificial thrill to be sure, but a thrill nevertheless.

The gambler, we must remember, has purposely placed himself in this position. If he stood outside the table and watched the dice being thrown, he could look at the scene with equanimity. He has nothing at stake, and therefore there is no thrill, since there is nothing to lose.

Nothing to lose! That is the key to participation and excitement in gambling for most of us. It is only when we have something of value to lose that we feel the thrill of gambling. And this thrill is in direct relation to the damage the loss will cost us. A man with an income of $20,000 a year would get bored playing penny-ante poker or betting dimes on a craps game. If he had $10 bets working for him, he'd be more involved. But take this same man with this same income and have him place $500 bets, and he is now in a heart-stopping situation. His blood pressure increases, his heart is pounding, his temples are throbbing, he is sweating heavily, and his attention is riveted on the game at hand. He has completely transformed himself from an idle spectator to an active participant; and yet, no one has forced him to gamble. But if he didn't gamble like this, he might never get that involved with anything at this intense level in his ordinary life outside the casino. For outside the casino, there probably is little opportunity for risk taking in his life.

Once money is involved, *money that can be lost,* any game involving an uncertain outcome over which we have no control becomes more intense. A good example is pro football. There are many reasons given for its hold on the public, but no officials of the sport want to admit that gambling on the game has led to a great deal of its popularity.

Again using the principle that the more the loss will hurt you, the more excitement you find in gambling, if you watch a pro football game on Sunday in the privacy of your living room, with a moderate bet on the game, you'll be somewhat involved. You'll want to see your team win, but if it loses, you won't lose that much.

However, if you have a dangerously large bet on the game, watching a football match this way is a wholly different experience. Now everything affects you. You are riveted to the set. Every fumble, every misplay affects you personally. You can't sit still; you fidget in your seat during uncomfortable moments involving your team on the field. For now you are deeply involved, not as a fan, but as someone who has a great deal to lose if your team loses.

And the bigger the bet and the more it will hurt you if you lose, the higher the excitement level till it can be heart-stopping. I recall watching a pro football playoff game with a man who had bet $50,000 on the game. We sat in the study of his house before a twenty-five-inch color TV set. Before the game started, there was already tension in the room; but he was comparatively relaxed because nothing had yet happened on the football field. Then the game began. I watched the gambler's face during the game. He showed extreme anxiety, a pulsation in his neck that became obvious, a red tinge covered his facial skin, and he displayed restless and jerky movements.

He tightened his lips and narrowed his eyes as the game went on. He was in the grip of frenzy. When it became apparent that his team was going to lose, his expression changed to open disgust. At the end of the third quarter, with his team trailing by three touchdowns, he cursed the team and life in general and snapped off the set, announcing that he was going to take a nap. He stopped off in the bathroom for a couple of tranquilizers, and I left the house.

Meanwhile, having no bet on the game, I watched with tranquility. I was rooting for his team to win, for I wanted to see him hold onto his $50,000; but I secretly thought the other team would win. We were watching the same game, yet one of us was near a nervous breakdown, all from the large bet. That's what accounted for our emotional gulf.

Finally, there are those people who gamble not because of the thrill involved but because they are under the delusion that this is an easy and quick way to earn money without really working for it. To make money at the tables or the racetrack, these gamblers prepare systems that they think will guarantee them an income for life. Or they feel that, having some knowledge of the games they'll be playing, luck will be on their side and see them through.

Perhaps these are the worst losers of all because they don't even get any excitement out of the betting. All they inherit is the anguish of losses. They don't realize that no system has been devised to beat any game that places the player at a disadvantage in terms of odds. And luck is an arbitrary element that can swing violently either way. They trust to luck because their skill at the games they play isn't sufficient to beat either the house or other opponents; and in the end, they're doomed to failure. But this doesn't stop their delusions. They save up money again after being wiped out, work out new systems and try once more, with the same miserable results.

All the reasons I've examined for gambling—the plunge into the unknown and uncertain world, the possibility of a big payoff for a small investment, the thrill of anxiety, the risk taking, the excitement of having bet money one can't afford to lose, and the delusion that this is an easy method of earning money—are wrong reasons for *the serious gambler* to be gambling.

This book is written for one express purpose: to show the serious gambler how to gamble and win. But before you can do that, you must know why you are gambling. And there should be only one reason to gamble, *and that is to win money.*

As you read on, you will discover the secrets of winning at gambling. Each of the chapters of this book will share this knowledge with you and prepare you to avoid the pitfalls that overcome so many of those who gamble and inevitably lose. It is not enough to know the games you should play and those you should avoid; you must learn to play and manage your money in an orderly and methodical manner. You must learn self-control and must be prepared mentally and psychologically to gamble to win. All these subjects will be covered thoroughly in future chapters.

III. CASUAL AND COMPULSIVE GAMBLING

There is nothing inherently wrong with casual gambling, for it is an activity enjoyed by millions of people. Most individuals want to get away from humdrum lives and business and work activities that aren't really rewarding. They want a change of pace, and they want excitement and adventure in their lives, and the gambling scene provides that instantly.

There is a vast difference between being a spectator and a bettor of the same event. The spectator may be interested or bored depending on the excitement generated by the event; but once a bet is made, there is a complete transformation in interest. Now the event is not only entertaining to the viewer who is betting but dramatic as well, and every nuance is watched over and examined by the bettor. There is instant drama in gambling, and that drama, missing so often from our lives, is relished by the occasional gambler. The small price exacted for this excitement, such as losing a little bet, seems fair in proportion to the pleasure received from the gambling.

In this book, I deal with serious gambling for the most part; but the occasional or casual bettor will have much to learn by reading these pages, such as the best games to play, the best bets, money management, and self-control. The only reason you should gamble seriously is to win money. While I can understand the desire of the casual gambler to add excitement to his or her life, that should never be the reason for serious gambling.

Most people like to gamble. They may go to a racetrack once in a great while; they may visit a gambling resort for a long weekend once a year; they may purchase state lottery tickets once a month. This activity is perfectly acceptable. It is when gambling moves from this casual basis to a compulsion that consumes all the gambler's time and energy that gambling can be real trouble. Serious gamblers are not necessarily compulsive gamblers, however. Far from it. Serious gamblers, who make intelligent studies of the games and strategies they will play and who maintain self-control and money management, are in no danger of becoming compulsive gamblers. In this chapter we're talking about people who have thrown self-control to the winds—whose interest is not in making money but having "action."

Like most other activities, indulgence in moderation is not harmful. The man or woman who has an occasional glass of wine or highball before or during dinner or has a drink or two at a social event is engaged in an innocent pastime. Drinking is casual and is done as a break from the ordinary patterns of everyday life. When drinking moves from there to the regular pattern of everyday life, when the intention is to search out places and opportunities to drink, then there is a problem.

From this problem, the drinker becomes obsessed with getting a drink and cannot live comfortably without constant use of alcohol. He or she needs a drink to wake up in the morning. If it is a choice between a bottle and a meal, the bottle takes precedence. Drinking becomes the standard aspect of the alcoholic's life, not a pleasure or pastime to be enjoyed occasionally. Somewhere between the problem and the compulsion, having a drink has ceased becoming fun or a relief. It is now an end in itself; it is everything.

The same thing happens in gambling. Like drinking, it can be very slow in developing, and usually the compulsive gambler, like the alcoholic, denies that it is a problem. It is something he or she can "stop at any time." But a compulsive activity is not that easy to stop.

Drinking can be fun and a break from the tension of life. Gambling can have that same cathartic effect. It is a good way to get rid of tensions, to yell and scream at the dog or horse races, the craps table, or merely to test one's skill at an occasional poker game. Casual players bet small stakes and win or lose a few dollars that they can well afford to spend in this manner. However, from that innocent position, gamblers might find that they want more than just fun. They may want not only a pleasurable excitement but the extreme thrill of having something important to lose, of taking a big risk.

Gamblers then purposely place themselves in situations where the outcome isn't fun anymore. Winning becomes a relief at *not having lost*. And here we have the statement that baffles so many people: gamblers don't really want to win. That is true. Gamblers, and I'm talking about problem and compulsive gamblers, don't want to win. On the other hand, they don't want to lose, either, because the money they hold onto allows them to have more action. When their money is gone, so is the action. And action creates the excitement they so desperately need.

A few years ago, I attended a conference on gambling in Las Vegas. It was held in Caesars Palace, and among those present was a friend of mine who is also a professional writer. We were standing in the casino after lunch one day, casually talking, when another man I knew, a local gambler, came by. I introduced the men to each other, and the gambler asked if we cared to join him for lunch. Since we had already eaten, we declined, and we talked for a few minutes, with the conversation turning to money.

"What would happen," I asked, "if someone came up to us and said, 'Here's $100,000. It's a gift. But I'd like to know what you're going to do with the money.'"

The writer said he'd invest it in AAA bonds at 8.5 percent interest, and this would take the pressure off him in terms of writing for a living. The gambler had quite a different answer. He'd take the money to the nearest craps table and really make some big bets. He didn't say he'd win money with the $100,000. No, that money represented several hours of heavy betting, at the limit.

I asked the gambler if he wouldn't invest it in some way to give him security of some kind. He looked at me as though I asked if he were flying to Mars that weekend. Security meant nothing to him; there was no excitement in security. That was for the tourists; the squares. What he craved was action. Action was living, it was excitement and thrills.

I've seen a lot of gamblers in my life, having lived for two periods of time in Las Vegas and having been on the gambling scene for a number of years as a writer, observer, and player myself. The problem gambler and the compulsive gambler have the same things in common. Gambling is their life, the high point of their existence, and in order to feed their desire to gamble, they need money.

The only difference between problem gamblers and compulsive gamblers, as far as I can see, is that problem gamblers don't fully recognize their own plight because they are still gambling with their own money. They haven't borrowed to the hilt yet. They've started lying to their families about where they've been, and they've taken away money from essential activities to use for gambling, but they still have some cash left. Compulsive gamblers are like heroin addicts. Most of their free time is spent searching for ways to get money to feed their habit. This is, however, an arbitrary distinction, and it may very well be that at the point where gambling is the most important activity in one's life, the person is a compulsive gambler, whether or not he or she has any money left.

A man or woman in the grips of a compulsion is a sad thing to see. The outcome is clear—loss, despair, bankruptcy. Gamblers know this as well, but they keep going despite this knowledge. They are already in the grip of something they cannot escape from without help. There are several organizations which give aid to such people, such as Gambler's Anonymous, which is based on the same principles as Alcoholics Anonymous; but before a person can be helped, he or she must recognize the problem and admit to being a compulsive gambler. That is sometimes the hardest thing to do.

Since you don't want to be a compulsive gambler, you must recognize the danger signs, and if they apply to you, you should immediately desist from betting and look for help. Here are the most common signs of a compulsive gambler.

- Money becomes just a vehicle for action, and money used for gambling has the highest priority, over family, food, and essentials.
- Instead of admitting that he or she is gambling, the gambler hides this fact from family and friends or passes off heavy gambling as casual gambling.
- In connection with the above, a pattern of lies controls his or her life, all relating to gambling and the money necessary to gamble with.
- As the money drains away, the gambler feels that bigger bets will make up the losses, and that sooner or later he or she will become "lucky" and get even.
- Borrowing or stealing money for gambling is not considered immoral or illegal because just as soon as he or she is even, it will all be paid back.
- After losing, the gambler feels guilty and swears off

gambling, but in a short while, he or she is overwhelmed by the same desire for action and once more starts gambling.

- A wild, optimistic excitement grips the gambler as he or she prepares to play, and all else is brushed from his or her mind.
- Money won at the gambling table is not considered spending money but fuel for further action and is not used to buy essentials. Only pressing debts that, if not paid off, will halt future sources of money for gambling are taken care of.
- The gambler avoids previous friends, family, and associates because they don't "understand" him or her any longer. The gambler becomes a loner; most gambling is done alone or with other compulsive gamblers.
- When someone close to the gambler points out his or her condition, the compulsive gambler denies it, reciting such statements as "all life is a gamble, anyway." When told he or she needs help, the gambler denies this, may become angry, and avoids contact with people who talk about this problem.

I have outlined ten basic points. Anyone fitting these categories is in serious trouble and should seek immediate help.

If you become a problem or compulsive gambler, you can never hope to become a winner. To gamble and win is not impossible, but you must never allow yourself to sink into a compulsion to gamble.

You can become a serious gambler, as this book points out, without becoming a compulsive gambler, for playing intelligently with proper strategy and money management is a sane approach to gambling—one that will enable you to gamble and win.

IV. HIDING FROM LIFE

A top-notch poker player once summed up the secret to his success, and he was very successful, winning over $100,000 a year at the game. He said, "Most poker players want to hide from life; they're in this special world of gambling, and they want action. They want to be in every pot; they want to gamble. The secret is to give them an excuse for action. Give them an excuse for calling your bet, even when you've got the living nuts. That's how I make my money."

The key phrase here is "hide from life." When a man or woman hides from the world, it generally is because of anxiety or depression, not wanting to face up to his or her life. Or they feel their life is empty of any excitement. Now there are many ways to relieve anxiety and just as many to get rid of depression, but gambling should not be one of them. The world abounds with exciting things to do; but to gamble for sheer excitement is the hallmark of the loser.

There is a great emphasis today on sports such as tennis

and running. They are fine for the body and mind. If the world is crowding you, how much better it is to get out and run for a while or take a long walk through a wooded area, feeling the blood coursing through your veins, feeling a natural high. This is just one example of what one might do when feeling restless. Some people read, others take photographs, others paint pictures. There are hobbies and crafts galore, all safe and all relaxing, and with some creative effort, quite stimulating. But gambling is not relaxing, and gambling is not the place to be when you feel anxious, depressed, or when craving excitement.

A dear friend of mine is a psychiatrist, and he once told me something that I've always remembered because his words saved me from a lot of grief and disaster. He said, "When you're depressed or anxious, don't make any decisions, because any decision you make under those conditions will tend to be destructive."

How true. We see it all the time in life, not only in gambling. When people are getting divorced, often one of the partners gives up everything under the strain of separation; and then, after a while, when things are back to normal, they rue the day they left themselves penniless. When a marriage breaks up or a love affair ends, who can think straight? That is the time to withdraw and pull oneself together; it is not the time for decisions affecting one's future.

Thinking back on those kinds of unhappy situations, we all shudder at our actions and our decisions. How destructive they were and how they still may haunt us today. It is just as destructive and dangerous to gamble under severe pressure or when depressed, troubled, or anxious. Your decisions are then tainted by your feelings, and at that point, you have no control over your feelings. My psychiatrist friend told me something else that always stayed with me. "You can rationalize reason, but always trust your feelings."

That is also true. I was a practicing lawyer at one time and handled a great many criminal cases. When I was before a jury, it was not reason that swayed them in deciding on a verdict; it was their feelings. Once you caught their feelings, they'd figure out a reason to vote the way they felt. It wasn't the other way around. Many so-called incompetent lawyers are not really incompetent; they just don't know what moves people. And their hapless clients end up behind bars.

What do I mean by feelings? Feelings are what we live with all the time—love, hate, sorrow, fear, joy, and anxiety are some of them.

Anxiety is a key one in terms of gambling. Too often you don't understand what anxiety is and may misinterpert your feelings, mixing up, for example, anxiety and tension. If you sat down to a big blackjack game, at a $25 table, and put down $2,000, knowing you were going to make bets ranging up to $150 at a time, I'm sure you'd be tense. Tension is not anxiety at this point. Tension is natural, and the right amount will rev you up for the game, will keep you sharp and alert. But anxiety, that overwhelming feeling of distress and uneasiness caused by impending danger or misfortune, is the great destroyer.

I'm now going to give three examples of situations I hope you never get into. However, many gamblers will recognize these situations and their own reactions. I call these "Hiding From Life" scenarios.

Scenario 1

You're in a poker game that's much too big for your financial resources, and you lied to your wife to get away for the evening. You don't know the players that well and are the friend of only one of them. You don't even know the game, seven-card stud, that well. But all week you've been feeling edgy and restless; your job is getting you down, and your wife has gained so much weight that you have very little interest in sex with her anymore. You just needed some kind of action, something different; when a pal from the office told you about this poker game, you were excited all day and couldn't wait for night to come. You vaguely remember having this same excited feeling when you were a young man, but then it had to do with dating a pretty girl.

After playing for a couple of hours, you're down several hundred dollars, money you can ill afford to lose. At this point you're sweating and uncomfortable and have a splitting headache. Every time you look at your cards you shudder, for you now realize *you don't want good cards.* Good cards will get you involved in a pot, and you've been beaten out of most of the pots you've been in with good cards.

You want terrible cards that will allow you to fold quickly or a monster hand, like three aces rolled up, so you can immediately have an overwhelming edge on the others. But you don't get those cards. On the very next hand, you have queens in the hole and an ace showing, and you must open the pot. After you bet, a king raises, and now you feel like throwing away your cards. You're afraid of the king and the raise; you have no confidence in the queens you hold. Why would the king raise with your ace showing? He must have a pair, or maybe he has the monster hand of three kings wired up right away. You look around the table and don't see another king. Two other players call the raise, and now its your turn again. You hem and haw, realizing all the other players are looking at you. They're all strangers except for your pal, and the holder of the king is also looking at you; he looks down at the chips you have left, and you know he knows you've been a big loser.

In your own mind at this moment, you're telling yourself "I can't think straight." And you can't. You pick up the chips to call the raise and look with dismay at your hands. They're shaking. You put down the chips and fold the cards, and as you do, you see the holder of the king smile ever so slightly. You hate him at this moment; you could kill him. You know in your heart he just bluffed you, and sure enough, the winning hand is jacks up; the holder of the king shows his hand at the end, and he never bought the fifth card to his flush.

You are no longer just tense or even anxious. You are in a state of panic and fear. You've lost touch with your feelings; they're out of control, and there's no guide for any moves in the game. And the money you've lost should have been used for the mortgage payment and some new clothing for the kids. It's time to cash in the chips and get out, because you can now be clairvoyant at this moment and know that sometime in the next couple of hours, you'll get up from this table broke, with empty pockets and a clouded mind.

Scenario 2

You go to the track in the morning, about 11 AM, having taken the day off from work, with a pleasant optimism coursing through your body. You have a few hundred bucks in your pocket, and instead of driving, you take the bus. It's a leisurely ride which will get you to the races in time for the daily double. On the way you read the past performance charts, study speed ratings, jockeys, weights, distances, and track conditions. Everyone on the bus seems in a good mood, and several people are joking around, to the amusement of the other passengers.

You feel just as cheerful. Your mind is very clear. By the time you're at the gates, you've made up your mind about selections. You'll bet a couple of daily doubles and put some money down on a horse in the first race that looks like a sure thing. Maybe you'll wheel this horse with all the others in the second race. Maybe not. But you know you have a winner.

You buy six daily double tickets and don't quite wheel your horse with all the horses in the second race, but you have the six best covered. Now you place a $20 bet on the horse you like in the first race.

You go to the men's room; you wander around looking for a good seat; you notice how green the infield looks, and how blue the sky is. You feel good. A day at the races was just what the doctor ordered. You feel relaxed for the first time in weeks. Your job has been lousy, your wife has recently been on your back, the kids have been particularly annoying, whining all week.

You light a cigarette and watch the tote board. Your horse is being bet; he is second choice at 5–2 and was only fourth choice in the morning line; so you feel more confident about your selection. Now he's 2–1.

The favorite is also 2–1 and has just a little more money bet on him for win than does your horse, but you note with satisfaction that there's more money bet on show on your horse. *He is your horse now.* You have a vested interest in his success. You like the way the odds are dropping. He's now the favorite at 2–1; the previous favorite has gone up to 5–2. This looks more like it. You suddenly rush to the betting window and place another $30 on your horse two minutes before post time. Now you have $50 on its nose, and another $12 in daily doubles backing him up.

At 2–1, you'll have $100 in profits and all those doubles working, and maybe you'll bet the four other horses in the second race so that you'll have them all wheeled one way or another.

You feel your heart beating a little faster as the bell rings and the announcer says, "It is now post time." Yes, this was the right place to be to get away from everything. In the fresh air, at the track. "And they're off," shouts the announcer, and your horse breaks fourth. Perfect. You look down at the *Racing Form.* He usually runs in front and it's a six-furlong race, but he's being rated today. At the turn into the stretch, he's third. OK. And now the crowd is screaming and you stand up to see what the yells are about. A horse is coming up on the outside.

"Come on, come on," the man next to you screams. "Come on," you scream, and now the horses are at the sixteenth pole, passing before your eyes. But where's your horse? He's not even among the first four. Finally, you see him straggle in, next to last.

You're stunned. What happened? The winner is a horse that pays 3–1, and suddenly you realize that the winner had been bet down the last minute from 6–1. You look at the program. He was 8–1 on the morning line. Why didn't you see that move? Why were you so blind?

Now there's no $100 profit to collect. You're out $62, and the admission was $3, and the bus ride and the program and the *Racing Form*. They all add up. You count your money. You have $230 left. There's still lunch to eat, but you're not hungry yet. Lunch can wait.

By the time the fifth race is over, you still haven't eaten. Now you have $90 left, and the cigarettes you've been smoking have made you dizzy and left a bad taste in your mouth. You just can't seem to pick a winner. You look at the *Racing Form*. You've circled a horse in the sixth race, but he's 8–5 on the board. You're down over $200 and you can't bet chalk now. You need a big win. You look at the program and look back at the board. Who's this 10–1 shot? He was 5–1 on the morning line and now he's 10–1. An overlay. If you bet $20 and he wins, you're just about even. It's a minute to post time. You go and bet the 10–1 horse and watch the favorite, who was your original choice, win by six lengths.

By the seventh race, you're down to $70 and desperate to get even. You ask yourself, "Why'd I come here in the first place? What excuse will I give the boss tomorrow? And my wife will nag me. And the kids . . ." You don't even want to think about all those things. You look at the program and the *Racing Form*, and it's all a blur. You can't pick a winner. You watch the board. You'll go with the smart money this time, just like in the first race. The smart money bet down that winner and you didn't even see it. But there seems to be no discernible pattern on the tote board, and you have to get even.

You know that 10–1 shots are out of the question. You can't bet on candidates for the glue factory, on platers that can't run faster than you can. You need a class horse, but at the right price. How about this 9–2 one? What does the handicapper say about him? "May need race." 9–2. If you bet $60, you'll collect $270 in winnings. That will leave you only $10 if you lose, but it doesn't matter now. This is the last race you'll be around for.

The hell with this track. Take the money and run after this win. You bet the horse and at the last minute he goes off at 7–2. So the smart money is on your horse. The race is run, and he comes in second by a length. He ran a good race; the smart money knew he was trying, but he just couldn't win. You leave the track, your stomach rumbling and your head racked with a headache, and there's an awful taste in your mouth.

On the bus home, you're in a completely different mood than the one you had on the way to the track. Your clothing feels damp and sticky, and you touch your shirt and realize you've been sweating fiercely. Everyone on the bus is silent, in contrast to the bus coming out to the track, where the men and women were animated and joking around. Now the passengers are listless, without exception. This is the bus after the seventh race; the loser's bus. Some people are dozing off, others are staring desolately out of the window. You are cranky and want to get off the bus, and you know you can't till it reaches the city, where you have nothing to look forward to.

Does this all sound familiar? It's a familiar story to a great many people. These are the people who are hiding from their real lives. They are burdened by depression and anxiety and are going to the wrong place to relieve that anxiety. After a few losses, their fragile mental makeup becomes unbalanced and they can't think straight. Every decision is wrong. There's no pattern to their decisions, which are whiplashed back and forth. One time they go with smart money; another with overlays. Sometimes the price is too high, sometimes it's too low. Sometimes form is important, other times the odds matter more. They're doomed to lose.

Scenario 3

You're at home, early Sunday morning, and the pro football team you root for will be on TV. Still a chance to make a bet with the bookie. You like the price. You had figured that your team would be a one touchdown favorite, and now you read the paper and find that they're 2 point underdogs. Impossible but true. Here's your chance to break your long losing streak betting on the pros.

You call the bookie and ask the latest line. He tells you that your team is now 3½ point underdogs. Even better. You lay $100 on the game. You'll be watching it on TV; you'll have a couple of beers and some snacks during the game. Perfect Sunday afternoon. Your wife is taking the kids to the in-laws. Just as well. You can relax and do your thing. You go to the kitchen for some coffee and cake and look at yourself in the mirror on the way. You've got a pot belly, and you know you can grab the fat around your waist with both hands and hold on. How much do you weigh? You haven't weighed yourself in a few months. You hesitate, go into the bathroom, and get on the scale. 198. 198! Impossible. You bend down to make sure the scale is on zero to start. It's true. Well, you're wearing a pair of pants and an undershirt. Take off, uh, four pounds. 194. But still, 194. When you were in college you weighed 155 at the most.

Troubled, you go into the kitchen and pour some coffee and open the refrigerator and cut a piece of cake, coffee cake with a cinnamon top, your favorite. What the hell. What difference is it going to make now? A couple of ounces one way or another. Back into the living room; 3½ point underdogs. You can't believe it. You go to the phone and call the bookie. You feel like hanging up when the phone is ringing because you know you should be taking it easy, not betting more dough. But you have that feeling. The bookie answers and you ask the point spread on the game. No difference, still 3½.

"Can I get 4?"

"How about a teaser?" he asks.

No, you just like that one team. You ask him to put you down for an additional, uh, four hundred. For a total of $500 on this game.

The bookie pauses. You're a hundred dollar bettor at the most. You want this much action? You owe him $500 now, after paying off close to a grand a couple of weeks ago. If you lose this, he informs you, it will put you over a grand again with the vig.

You hesitate. But 3½ points; it's a steal.

"Make it $500."

"It's a bet," you're told.

You hang up. That's why you bet $500, didn't the stupid bookie know that? To get even and wipe out that debt. Still, it's the biggest bet you've made all season—$500. You call the bookie right back and ask if there are any injury reports, because if there are, you want to cancel the bet.

"No, no injuries on the team."

"OK, the bet's on," you say and hang up.

You have another slice of cake and more coffee, and then at lunchtime you fix a sandwich of cold cuts and then at 1 PM turn on the game.

It's raining slightly in Minnesota, but your team plays well in the rain. A scoreless tie would be OK; also it would beat the spread, and it's hard to score in the rain. But you now remember that they have overtime, and it's better if the score is 7–6 either way, as long as your team beats the spread.

You're a little tense, but you know your team. They can not only keep the score close, they can win this game. The players are introduced during your idle musings. The national anthem is played; the game is ready to begin. Your team wins the toss. Good. They'll receive. Things are already going your way. But on the kickoff, you're out of your chair, screaming. The stupid receiver fumbled, and there's a pileup, and it's Minnesota's ball. No! Your team is now defending on its four-yard line. Jesus Christ, what miserable luck!

And in two plays you're behind 7–0, and the game isn't even a minute old. Well, one touchdown and you're back in business. A beer would taste good now, and by the fourth beer it's the second quarter and still no change in the score. By halftime, still no change. Just one touchdown by your team, that's all you need. During halftime you wander around the house, restless, not knowing what to do. You feel like getting out, doing something physical, but even walking upstairs to your bedroom for a clean handkerchief causes you to pant for breath.

The second half begins with you planted in your easy chair, another beer at hand. No change for a few minutes, then suddenly Minnesota intercepts and has a first down on your team's 12-yard line. Hold! Damn it, hold! Defense! But your screams are to no avail. Minnesota 14, your team 0. When the score is 21–3, with four minutes left in the game and Minnesota driving again, you feel sick to your stomach from all the food and beer you had. And that $500 bet. Where are you going to grab this $1,000 to pay off the bookie? You got the other money from the finance company, but what about this thousand? You can't even think straight. Why didn't you leave the lousy bet at $100? Why'd you have to make the other call? Why didn't you leave well enough alone? Regrets, headaches, you can feel your heart beating fast. And out of shape and stuck in the house. The walls feel like they're closing in.

I could go on and on with these horrible examples, since

they're all true and played over in various ways every day by thousands of gamblers. These people are caught up in gambling fever, and they look for excitement out of the regular course of their life. They are, as the man said, "hiding from life."

If I were to lump all three gamblers together and state one truth about them, I'd say they shouldn't be gambling in the first place. Gambling, unfortunately, attracts people like this, who are miserable in their own worlds and who look for the forced anxiety of betting, which passes for excitement in their dreary lives. That's not the reason to gamble. That's just the reason for losing. Don't retreat from life when gambling . . . instead, treat gambling as just one other aspect of your life.

If you want to make it as a gambler, the first thing you should do is examine your motives for gambling. Are you in it just for thrills? Then get out. Are you in it so you can feel your heart pound as the dice are rolled, or as the horses come down the stretch at the track, or watching the football game, knowing that you have an enormous bet (for you) on the outcome and you'll be at the edge of your seat for the whole game? Get out. I can't state this strongly enough. *Get out.* That's not what gambling should be all about; for these thrills and anxiety provoking situations are for the loser, not for the winner.

Serious gambling should never be something you do to hide from life. *Gambling is something you should do to win.* Unless you're in it to win, don't gamble!

THE GAMES

V. CASINO GAMES TO AVOID

American casinos offer a wide variety of gambling games. Craps and blackjack, which are the basic table games, are the most popular and get the biggest play in terms of money bet. Then there are the other two table games; roulette and baccarat (also mini-baccarat), slot machines, and keno. Finally, some casinos have minor games such as Chuck-A-Luck and the Money Wheel. Several casinos also offer poker, but this game will be discussed in the poker section.

Before we discuss the play of the various games, let's determine which games you should avoid and which you should participate in. By avoiding those games in which the odds against you are prohibitive or in which you have little chance of winning, no matter how attractive the game, you are already on your way to becoming a winner. First, we'll look at the games to avoid.

Chuck-A-Luck and the Money Wheel

Both of these games are rarely seen in casinos, but occasionally they may be found, with the dealer trying to get some action going. Chuck-A-Luck is played with three dice in a wired cage. The cage is flipped over by the dealer, and you bet on a layout featuring the numbers 1–6. If the dice show your number one time, the payoff is even money. If your number appears on two dice, the payoff is 2–1, and if all three dice come up with your number, the payoff is 3–1. The house edge is over 7½ percent, and this archaic game should be avoided by any serious player.

The Money Wheel is a huge wheel with slots corresponding to money payoffs. You bet on a layout which shows the following denominations of U.S. currency—$1, $2, $5, $10, and $20. There is also a joker or house number which pays off at $40–1. If the wheel comes up on a slot corresponding to the denomination you bet on, you are paid off in that amount. For instance, if you bet on the $5 on the layout and the $5 comes up, you get $5 for your $1 bet. The odds favor the house an average of 22 percent on this game, and these odds are prohibitive. Any player with any sense should stay away from this game.

Keno

Keno is one of the oldest of the casino games, and its history can be traced back almost 2,000 years to the Han Dynasty in China, where the game was used to raise money and provisions for the army.

The earliest form of the game contained 120 Chinese ideograph characters, drawn from the *Thousand Character Book,* which was a classic known to most literate Chinese. After a while, the number of characters dropped to 90. Then, when it was introduced into America by Chinese immigrants, it was further reduced to 80 characters.

It spread in popularity in America, and many non-Chinese started to play the game. It is a game in which huge payoffs are possible for a small wager, and this has always been a popular concept among lower-income workers. Since the non-Chinese couldn't differentiate between the Chinese characters, Arabic numerals, from 1–80, were introduced.

When Nevada legalized gambling, the game of keno was introduced as "race horse keno." Each ball contained not only a number, but the name of a horse. However, due to United States government regulations, the race horse aspect was dropped, and in 1951 the game was officially changed to keno.

It is played in practically all the major casinos in Nevada. Several of the more plush hotels, particularly on the Strip in Las Vegas, have done away with lounge shows in order to convert these areas to keno lounges.

The game is very simple to play. There are 80 numbers to choose from, and the player may select from 1 to 15 numbers to bet on. If a certain number is bet on, and it "catches" or is selected, the player wins. If several numbers are bet on, and some of these "catch" the player also wins. Betting is done in increments of either 70¢ or $1, depending on the casino.

You select your numbers by marking a ticket with a crayon or pen, crossing out the numbers you choose. If you bet on one number, the payoff is 2–1 if the number comes up or catches. The more numbers you bet on, the higher the possible payoffs. For example, betting 70¢ on a 15-number ticket, if 11 catch, the payoff is $1,500; if 12 come up, the payoff is $5,000; and if all 15 catch, the payoff is $25,000. With these huge payoffs for so small an investment, you can readily see why keno is so popular.

The numbers are selected by casino personnel. An operator forces Ping-Pong balls, each with its own number corresponding to a number between 1–80, through what is known as a "goose," a long cyclindrical plastic tube. There is room for twenty of these Ping-Pong balls, each with separate numerals, and the player wins or loses depending on what numbers have been chosen. All results are flashed on electric sign boards, and players can see the results from practically anywhere in the casino, including the restaurants.

I have been discussing what are known as "straight tickets," where from 1 to 15 numbers can be selected, but there are various other tickets, some of them very complicated, called "combination" or "way" tickets. However, I'm not going to dwell on the intricacies of the game, except to state that in all bets on keno, the house has an advantage of over 20 percent.

This is a fun game to play for 70¢ while having dinner in a casino, particularly if the conversation at the table is boring. I've been with people who played it at mealtime, and their discussion invariably centered on how they'd be spending the $25,000, which of course they didn't win.

Keno is primarily a game to be played this way, for fun, if you want to wager a couple of dollars and enjoy the prospect of talking about a big win, but it should never be played for serious money. Losses can mount up steadily, and it's not unusual to see people sitting in the keno lounge hour after hour, betting several dollars on each game, and ending up a day's play with losses in the hundreds of dollars.

It's a very seductive game because of the large possible payoffs and attracts, for the most part, those people who want a lot for a little. But you should know that when this is offered, someone must pay heavily; and it is the gambler who pays, for the house edge is horrendous. Avoid this game except as an occasional pastime.

Slot Machines

Slot machines are a big moneymaker for the casino because very little maintenance is required for these machines, and one change girl and one mechanic can usually handle a great number of slots. Slot machines are basically built to pay off in two ways. First, there is the standard machine, which has a list of payoffs on its face. The jackpot is predetermined and unchanging. The second kind of machine is the "progressive" machine, and the jackpot increases steadily with each play.

No matter what kind of machine you play, whether it is progressive or straight, the house edge is figured mathematically in advance, and there is no way you're going to overcome this disadvantage. On the straight machines, there will be many small payoffs and a few large ones, but the payoffs will come dribbling down with regularity.

On the progressive machines, with their larger jackpots, the payoffs will be infrequent, with the expectation of the one big jackpot hitting, but this jackpot comes rarely, for only one pull out of many thousands will produce it.

The standard calculations are made by the casinos as follows. There are generally three reels on each machine, and there are 20 symbols on each reel. Thus, there are a possible 8,000 combinations before they are all depleted. Eight thousand coins can be fed into the machine due to the formula (20^3), and if the machine pays off 6,400 at the end of the cycle, the house will have retained 1,600 and will have a 20 percent profit. Should the machine retain only 800 coins for the casino, then the house would have a 10 percent advantage or profit, and so on.

The machines are set up for their payoffs in advance by the mechanic, and unless you want to break the law and tamper with them, there is no way to change their payoffs, which favor the house an average of 16 percent.

The machines are very popular. Some payoffs on the progressive machines, particularly the well-publicized ones, where the machine takes in multiple dollars as its standard coins, can be astronomical, running into the hundreds of thousands of dollars. About a year ago, a man won over $300,000 on such a machine at the MGM Grand in Las Vegas, and similar payoffs have been recorded in some of the big hotels in northern Nevada.

These machines are the exception, of course. The average slot machine is geared to the small bettor, who buys a couple of dollars worth of nickels and plays the machine for awhile, generally until the nickels run out, which they invariably do. Nickel or 5¢ machines are still the most numerous and the most popular. There are also 10¢ and 25¢ machines, but they don't get the play of the nickel ones.

Recently, the Bally Company, which manufactures most of these machines, introduced the dollar machines into many of the Nevada casinos. These machines are owned by Bally and leased to the casinos and are unique in that these are the only machines which actually show the house edge. A sign near the machines states that the machines are "96 percent or 97 percent in your favor" which means that the house edge is either 4 percent or 3 percent.

For many years, the casinos have been trying to upgrade the play on slots from 5¢ to higher denominations, and the popularity of the dollar slots have finally done the trick. They get enormous play and are kept together in certain sections of the casino, called "carousels."

How to beat the slots? It's difficult on all but the dollar machines. For one thing, you're never told the actual house edge, which may vary from 6 percent up to 30 percent, depending on the greed of the casino. The only way to know the casino advantage is to either be a slot mechanic or to see the computer runs on each machine, which shows the actual take. All this is further complicated by the fact that the casinos don't have a standard edge for all their machines within a casino. They have a "slot mix," not only of various denominations of machines, but of different percentages on each machine.

The casino personnel know that most people like to play two machines at one time, and so they may set the payoffs on the machines in tandem. One machine will be "loose," the players' term for a machine that pays off well, and the one next to it will be "tight," so that, as one pays off, the other is taking back all the profits.

No machine, in any casino, is set at even money or gives the player any advantage over the house. And no casino is obligated to list the edge it has on any of its machines. There is a general rule of thumb to be followed by people who like to play the slots; play in those casinos where slots are featured as the main game. There the payoffs are better and the slots much looser. Also, since slot players are catered to, they may be given gifts as well as snacks and free drinks.

The more luxurious hotels don't care to attract the slot players in hordes, and so cater to those gamblers who play the basic table games. In the Las Vegas Strip hotels, the payoffs are much tighter, and the house probably takes in between 16 percent and 20 percent as its profit.

In the new Atlantic City casinos being opened, an informant tells me that the payoffs on the slots will give the house an average 16 percent edge. This is a big bite, of course, and eventually it wipes out the player's bankroll.

If you want to try your luck at slots, your best bet is to play the dollar machines at the carousels, where you know the actual edge that the house has. Then, to give yourself *an edge,* tip the change girl in charge of the carousel, and ask her which machines haven't hit a jackpot in a while, and take her advice and play those machines. I've done well in my spare time following this method, and you should also.

Otherwise, unless you want to kill some time and have some fun with a couple of dollars, don't bother with the slots.

There's no way to beat them in the long run. You can do what my mother does. If she puts in a nickel and two come out, that's it. She takes her nickel profit and leaves.

Baccarat

Baccarat is much more popular in Europe because the European version allows the players to retain the bank and book bets themselves. In the American version of the game, the house books all bets, whether the gambler wants to wager on Bank or on Player.

Baccarat is a mindless game, one in which the only decisions are whether to bet on Bank or Player and how much to bet. There are no other independent decisions to be made by the participants.

If the Player hand wins, then the bets on Player are paid off. If Bank wins, then those bets are paid off, but 5 percent is deducted from the winning bet as a house commission. The commissions are added up by two dealers, one for each side of the table, and after the cards are reshuffled for a new series of deals, the commissions are then collected from the players.

The 5 percent commission is deducted from all winning Bank bets because, by the rules of the game, the Bank bet has an advantage over the Player bet. After the 5 percent commission is taken off, the house has an advantage of approximately 1.3 percent over the Player bet and 1.2 percent over the Bank bet; but it always has an advantage, no matter what bet is made.

The baccarat table is set up so that twelve people may play, six on either side of the dealers. The participants sit while playing, and a shoe, containing eight decks of cards is passed around the table, and can be handled by each of the gamblers. A gambler may hold the shoe at his or her option, since there is no benefit from holding the shoe. Usually, a bettor playing Bank holds the shoe until the Bank bet finally loses, and then the shoe moves on to the next player in a clockwise fashion.

While holding the shoe, the player deals out four cards from the shoe, two to the callman, who stands facing the other dealers, and two to himself as the nominal bank. The callman traditionally gives his cards to the person betting the most on Player, for these are the Player's cards. After the bettor on Player turns them over, he returns them to the callman, who places them in the box marked Player. Then the holder of the shoe turns over his two cards and gives them to the same callman, who places them in the Bank box. All this ritual means nothing at all and is traditional. The callman announces the values of the two hands, determines which hand should receive additional cards according to a prescribed and rigid set of rules governing baccarat and then which hand is the winner. After the winning hand is announced, bets are paid off, and commissions, if any, are deducted.

All decisions made in this game are subject to inexorable and printed rules, and the rules are printed on a card for any of the participants to examine, if they have any questions about a dealer's move.

The object of the game is to get a 9 or as close to 9 as possible. After the two hands are added up, the one closest to 9 wins. If two hands are equal in points, it is a standoff and no money changes hands. For purposes of baccarat, all face cards, jacks, queens, and kings, as well as tens, are counted as zero and have no value as points. All other cards have the same numerical value as the number of spots on their faces. For example, an ace is counted as 1, a five as 5, and so forth.

Since the highest possible total is 9, any hand containing more than 9 points is reduced by 10 points by removing the first digit from the total. To make this clear, suppose that a hand contains 8, 5 for a total of 13. The first digit or ten is subtracted from this hand and it now has a value of only 3. Likewise, 8, 7 would only total 5, since 10 is subtracted from the 15 original total. And 9, 9 would total 8.

An immediate total of 8 or 9 is called a "natural." This hand wins without any further cards drawn. If two hands have naturals, the 9 hand wins over the 8 hand. If both are tied with 8s or 9s, then the hand is a standoff, and no bets are paid off. On most other hands, an additional card may be drawn under the rules of baccarat, and the three-card total is added up in the same manner as the original two-card total. Thus 5, 5, 6 would be a 6, and 5, 5, jack would be zero.

The American casinos endeavor to give the game a certain aura by all this ritual. On the Strip in Las Vegas, the baccarat area is usually cordoned off, and the game is played with higher limits than the other table games. The usual baccarat limits are $20 to $2,000. This higher limit and the exclusive area used for the game, together with the custom of dressing baccarat dealers in tuxedos, gives the game a certain glamor which it wouldn't otherwise have, for it is basically a mindless and dull game.

Some of the downtown Las Vegas casinos and some casinos in northern Nevada play a version of this game called mini-baccarat. The same rules prevail, but there is only one dealer, dressed like all the other dealers, and all commissions for winning bets on Bank are paid immediately. The minimum bet is usually $2, making it much the same as other table games. It is played infrequently by gamblers, and it is unusual to see more than one mini-baccarat table in any casino.

Although the house edge is low, the game tends to be boring and slow, unless big money is involved in the betting. But then, any game in which a player wants to wager thousands on the turn of a card can be an exciting one. However, for most gamblers, the only way to win at baccarat, that is, win large amounts, is to bet large amounts. I feel that this is another game to avoid, unless you want to feel part of the so-called "glamour" of the game, and want to bet a minimum of $20 on a decision over which you have no control. There are better games to play, with lower odds favoring the house, such as craps and blackjack. Craps has more action and a greater chance to win a lot of money in a shorter period of time, without making huge bets. And blackjack is a game in which the player actually has an edge over the house.

Roulette

This is another casino game that is much more popular in Europe. Besides being the traditional gambler's game in European casinos, the European version gives the gambler a better break. There is only one zero on the wheel, as opposed to the American wheel with two zeroes. European wheels also have the *en prison* rule. This rule allows a bet on any of the even money choices to be imprisoned for an additional spin if the zero comes up. With these two rules in force, the European game gives the house an edge of approximately 1.35 percent as against the American house edge of 5.26 percent.

There are a few casinos in America where a single zero is used, but there is no casino in Nevada allowing the *en prison* rule. When a single zero is used, the house edge is reduced to 2.70 percent.

There are 36 numbers on the roulette wheel, running from 1–36, but placed in a random fashion on the wheel. Half the numbers are black, and the other half, red. Then there are the house numbers, 0 and 00, making 38 numbers in all. The 0 and 00 are in green and are not figured in any bets involving even or odd, high or low, or red or black. When the ball lands in a 0 or 00 slot, all these even-money bets are automatic losers. If a player has bet on any number other than 0 or 00, those bets are also losers. The payoff on all bets is governed by the fact that there are 38 numbers all together, with only 36 of them active on most bets, and thus the house has an advantage of 5.26

percent. There is a five-bet, betting 0, 00, 1, 2, and 3, in which the house advantage is even greater; but no matter what kind of bet you make in roulette, the house edge remains the same, except for that five-bet.

Roulette in American casinos is handled by only one dealer, while the European game involves several dealers. The usual minimum bet in American casinos is anywhere from 25¢ to $2, and even where you can bet 25¢ on any one kind of bet, you must place at least $2 in total bets on the layout at one time.

The game is played leisurely, with the dealer spinning the wheel after all bets are down. You can bet on individual numbers, on adjacent numbers, on corners, on six or eight contiguous numbers, on dozens, on columns, and on the even-money bets. There is no limit to the number of or variety of bets you may make. There is usually a house limit on individual and even-money bets, but other than the house limit, a gambler can place chips all over the layout. Since several players may participate at one time, Nevada casinos issue special roulette chips of different colors, an individual color for each player.

No matter what kinds of bets are made, the house edge of 5.26 percent hangs over the game. This is too great a disadvantage for a player to overcome; so my advice is to avoid American roulette wheels.

VI. CRAPS—A GAME TO PLAY

This is the fastest and most exciting gambling game in American casinos. Officially it is known as bank craps, because the house books all bets, whether the gambler bets with or against the dice. Since there is a slight advantage to betting against the dice, or betting wrong, the casino, in order to keep its edge on every bet, bars the 12 in Las Vegas and the 2 in northern Nevada. By taking away this bet from wrong bettors, the house has an approximate advantage of 1.4 percent on any line bet, right or wrong.

Bets are not limited to line bets, however. On a craps layout there are a great many bets available to the player, but most of them are bad bets. Some of these bets depend on a complete series of rolls, while others are won or lost on a single roll of the dice. We'll discuss all these bets after describing the game itself.

Craps is played with two dice, each perfect cubes, and each numbered with from one to six dots. The possible combinations these two dice together can make is 36, and these 36 combinations determine the odds and payoffs in craps. The lowest number that can be rolled with two dice is 2, and the highest, 12. There are slang terms for practically every number. Two is known as "snake eyes," and 12 is known as "box cars," but in the casinos, both are simply "craps," losers on the pass line.

The basic game is divided into two parts. First, there is the initial or come-out roll. Before the roll, bets can be made on whether the dice will pass, or win, or whether they won't win, or don't pass. Since a don't-pass bet wins for wrong bettors, to avoid confusion, we'll refer to pass-line bets as betting right, and to don't-pass bets as betting wrong. By using the terms right and wrong, we are making no moral judgment, just giving them a nomenclature we can work with. About 90 percent of the bettors bet with the dice, or bet right, though there is no theoretically greater advantage to betting right.

On the come-out roll, there is an immediate decision in favor of the pass-line or right bettor if the dice come up 7 or 11. This is an immediate loss for the don't-pass or wrong bettor. At the craps table, all bettors are subject to the roll of the dice by the roller or shooter. His or her roll determines all bets as winners or losers.

If the dice come up either 2, 3, or 12, all numbers known as "craps," on the initial or come-out roll, then this is an immediate loss for the right or pass-line bettor, and an immediate win for the don't-pass or wrong bettor, with the exception of the 12. I mentioned before that the house bars either a 12 or 2. For purposes of this section, we'll go with the Las Vegas rules and bar the 12. Thus, if a 12 is rolled on the come-out roll, the right bettors lose, but the wrong bettors merely have a standoff, neither winning nor losing.

So first, let's summarize the come-out roll's immediate decisions. For the right bettor, a 7 or 11 wins, and a 2, 3, or 12 loses.

For the don't-pass or wrong bettor, a 2 or 3 wins, a 12 is a standoff, and the 7 or 11 loses.

If any other number is rolled on the come-out roll, that number is then known as the point. The point numbers are 4, 5, 6, 8, 9, or 10. If one bets pass-line or right, and a point number is rolled on the come-out roll, then that number must be repeated before a 7 is rolled for the right bettor to win. Suppose the point is 5. If it is repeated before a 7 is rolled, the right bettor wins the bet on the pass-line, and, conversely, the wrong bettor loses.

If one bets don't-pass or wrong, then, if a 7 is rolled before the point is repeated, the wrong bettor wins, and the pass-line or right bettor loses. Let's show an imaginary series of rolls to see how this happens.

The come-out roll shows an 8. Now, an 8 must be repeated before a 7 is rolled for the right bettors to win. The next roll is a 5, and the roll after that is a 9. Neither roll means anything as far as the point 8 is concerned. Then a 2 is rolled. The 2 is not a losing number now, for this is not the come-out roll. Then an 11 is rolled. This is not a winning number for right bettors for the same reason. Then a 7 is rolled. This ends the roll. The right bettors lose their bets because the 7 came up before the 8 was repeated, and the wrong bettors win their bets.

The 7 can be made in 6 different ways, while the 6 and 8 can only be made five ways. The 5 and 9 can be made four ways, and the 4 and 10 only three ways. Since any point number has fewer ways to be made than the 7, the odds are against any point number being repeated before the 7 is rolled. Since the 6 or 8 can be made in five ways, the odds against a 6 or 8 are 6–5. The odds against the 5 or 9 are 3–2, and the odds against the 4 and 10 are 2–1.

After a point is rolled on the come-out roll, the players have the option of making odds bets to take advantage of the odds against points being repeated. For example, suppose the point is 4. Pass-line or right bettors can now make an equivalent bet on the odds bet. If they bet $10 on the pass-line, they now can bet $10 more on the odds bet. They do this by putting $10 worth of chips behind the original bet. If the point is made, they'll collect $10 for the pass-line bet at even money and $20 for the odds bet at the true odds of 2–1. There is nothing on the layout to indicate this bet, but it is allowed at all American casinos and should be made by all right bettors, since the house has no edge on this bet (that's why its called a "free-odds" bet); and by making this bet, players reduce the house edge against them on an overall basis from 1.4 to 0.8 percent.

Wrong bettors can make an odds bet, but instead of taking odds of 2–1 on the point 4, they lay odds of 2–1. Thus, if they've bet $10 on the don't-pass line, they can now make an additional bet of $20 on the free odds bet, laying 2–1 against the 4 being repeated before the 7 comes up. These are correct odds, on which the house has no advantage, and it reduces the house odds or advantage from 1.4 to 0.8 percent for wrong bettors.

If a bettor is allowed to take or lay double odds, the house edge is further reduced to 0.6 percent. A double odds bet is made by betting twice the amount on the free odds bet as was made on the pass-line or don't-pass bet. A player who bets $10 on the pass-line could make a $20 odds bet at the correct odds. And if the point was 4, for example, a wrong bettor could now bet $40 at 2–1 against the 4 being made. The $40 bet is made against $20, and if the 7 was rolled before the 4 was repeated, the wrong bettor would win $10 on the don't-pass bet and $20 on the free odds bet.

I emphasize odds bets because they are the key to winning at craps and should always be given or taken, as the case may be. The house, to repeat, has no advantage on these bets, and they substantially reduce the casino edge in all cases.

In addition to pass-line or don't-pass bets, there is one other kind of bet intelligent craps players should make and that is a come or don't-come bet. This bet cannot be made on the come-out roll; but, once a point is established, this bet can be laid.

Suppose the point is 8. On the very next roll, players may make a come bet if they are betting the pass-line or a don't-come bet after they have made a don't-pass bet. They put their chips into the correct betting box, marked either "Come" or "Don't Come."

Let's assume that you have bet the pass-line for $10 and the point is 6. You have made a $10 free odds bet, and now before the next roll, you place $10 in the "Come" box. The come bet is the same as the come-out roll pass-line bet, for it allows you, as a right bettor, to make a series of the same types of bets. If, on the next roll, a 7 or 11 is rolled, you win your come bet; and if a 2, 3, or 12 is rolled, you lose the come bet. Any other number is then moved to an appropriate place on the layout, and the right bettor can also make an odds bet on this come bet.

As a don't-pass bettor you can make additional don't-come bets and give odds against the numbers that are rolled being repeated, just as you can on the don't-pass line. Any of these come or don't-come bets, with the player taking or giving odds, gives the house no more than 0.8 percent as its edge. And if the house permits double odds, its edge is reduced to 0.6 percent.

To illustrate how come bets are made, let's follow a full roll, where you as a right bettor bet pass-line and make two come bets. All your bets are for $10, and you take single odds on all your bets. The come-out roll is 6, and that becomes the point. Having bet $10 on the pass-line you now bet $10 on the free odds bet at 6–5. You now put $10 in the come box, and the next roll is a 5. Your chips are moved to the (5) box, and you give the dealer another $10 as odds on the 5 at 3–2. Then you place another $10 in the come box. The next roll is an 8. The chips are removed by the dealer to the (8) box, and you hand the dealer $10 as a free odds bet.

At this point, you have three numbers working for you; the 6 as a point and the 5 and 8 as come bets. If any of these numbers is repeated before the 7 shows on the dice, you collect your bet, which includes a line or come bet plus the odds. For example, if the next roll is a 5, you collect $10 on the 5 as a come bet, and $15 as your odds bet, plus your original bets back. Now you have only the pass-line and one come bet working. If a 7 is now rolled, you lose both your line and come bet that is working, plus the odds bets.

If the don't-pass bettor makes a don't-pass bet of $10 and the same 6 is rolled as a point, he may lay $12 as his free odds bet at 6–5. Then he makes a don't-come bet and if the 5 is rolled, he can lay $15 as a free odds bet. If the next roll is an 8, he again lays $12 on the free odds bet after betting $10 in the don't-come box. Now if the 5 is repeated, he loses his don't-come bet of $10, plus $15 as his free odds bet for a total loss of $25. However, if the next roll is a 7, he wins his don't-pass bet and collects $20 for that bet and another $20 for his don't-come bet on the 8. He would net $15 for his don't-pass and don't-come bets, giving the odds.

Betting pass-line and taking odds, then making two come bets also taking odds, or betting don't-pass, laying odds, making two don't-come bets and also laying odds are the only intelligent bets to make on the craps layout. Avoid all other bets. Making these recommended bets at single odds gives the house only 0.8 percent advantage and making them at double odds gives the house only an 0.6 percent edge.

Any other bet that is made on the layout gives the house a greater advantage over the player, and thus should be avoided. By making these bets, players can, with a good winning streak, make a lot of money and can weather many bad losing streaks because they are giving the house so little in the way of an advantage. For gamblers wanting quick action in an exciting game with the chance of a big win, craps is the ideal game to play.

I could discuss all the other possible bets in detail, but I will simply state them, for they are all bad bets. The center, or proposition, bets give the house anywhere from 9.09 to 16.7 percent as an edge. Avoid the Field bets, which give the house either a 5.55 or 2.77 percent edge, depending on whether a 12 is paid off at 2–1 or 3–1. Avoid the Big 6 and Big 8 bets, which give the house 9.09 percent.

Finally, there are the place bets. After the come-out roll, a gambler may make bets on 4, 5, 6, 8, 9, or 10 as place bets, by betting a minimum of $5 on all numbers but the 6 and 8, and a minimum of $6 on these numbers. The house advantage on place bets runs from 1.52 percent on the 6 and 8 to 6.67 percent on the 4 and 10; so it pays to avoid these bets.

Now we'll deal with the strategy necessary to beat craps and come out a winner. The strategy can be accomplished by betting either right or wrong; it is immaterial and depends on the outlook of the player. Some people don't like to bet against the dice (wrong), feeling they are being pessimistic by doing so. Or they don't like to bet more money than they'll receive back, which will happen if they lay free odds against the points. So they prefer to become right bettors.

On the other hand, there are players who enjoy going against the general mood of the table and betting wrong. Since most people bet right, they feel they're not part of the mob. Or they feel the dice are "cold" more often than they are "hot" and thus feel that betting wrong is the best policy.

Either way is correct, just so long as bettors follow our advice, limit their bets, and always take or lay the free odds, reducing the house advantage to either 0.8 or 0.6 percent depending on whether or not they are permitted single or double odds.

If possible, take or lay double odds. It always pays to reduce the house advantage to the bare minimum, and by using double odds, you can win money much more quickly if the dice go your way. If only single odds are permitted, take or lay them, for the house has no advantage on these free odds bets.

Now, for the strategy. First, we'll deal with pass-line or right betting. If only single odds are permitted, bet three units if possible, with a minimum of $5 on the pass-line. I suggest three units or multiples thereof, because with single odds, the house will permit 5 units to be bet on the free odds bets if the 6 or 8 is the point or a come number, and this is to the advantage of the player.

After making the pass-line bet, take the odds on whatever point is rolled. Then make two come bets and take the odds on each come bet, all that is allowed. If a come bet repeats, and your bet is paid off, then make another come bet, for you always want two come bets working.

If double odds are allowed, it is no longer necessary to bet in multiples of three units because you can get double odds on all your bets; but bet at least $5, so that you can get 6–5 on the 6 and 8. Again, use the same strategy as with single odds bets. If a come bet is repeated and paid off, make another come bet. Keep two come bets working at all times.

If you are a wrong bettor, then bet at least $5 on the don't-pass line and on the don't-come bets, so that you can lay 6–5 odds on the 6 and 8. If a 5 or 9 is either the point or come bet and you've bet $5, you will be permitted to lay $9–$6 against these numbers as a free odds bet. This is to your advantage.

In double odds games, bet double the odds against any point number or come bet. Make one don't-pass bet and then two don't-come bets, just as you would in single odds games. If a come number repeats and the don't-come bet is wiped off, then let it stay off. Don't make another don't-come bet. This will protect you in case you run into a hot roll, where a great many numbers are made. Once a 7 is rolled, you will win both your don't-pass and your don't-come bets, together with the free odds bets.

This is a simple but very effective method of beating craps. You'll be betting intelligently and giving the house only a minimal advantage. You'll be known as a "tough" bettor, because the casino can't get too much from you at the average game; and, if you have a good streak, you can really take a lot of money away from the house.

Betting this way will make you a winner, but you must leave the table with winnings in order to be a winner. Remember this. In another chapter, we discuss when and under what circumstances to leave the craps table while winning.

VII. BLACKJACK

Blackjack, or 21, as it is sometimes called, is unique among casino games in that it is the only game in which the player has, at times, an advantage over the house. Unlike such games as roulette, where the wheel has no memory and where the game's rules are such that the house always has an advantage over the player, in blackjack you're dealing with the composition of a deck of cards, and the odds change as the cards are dealt out.

The changes brought about by the depletion of the deck of cards will determine whether the house or the player has the advantage. In order to know this, it is necessary to "count cards," but this doesn't mean remembering every card already played. There are various methods of card counting to ascertain if the player or the house has the edge on the forthcoming deal, and we'll cover a simplified version in this section.

The fact that blackjack can be beaten by the player has been worked out by computer studies; the original research was made by Julian Braun and then popularized by Edward Thorp in his fascinating book *Beat the Dealer*. In this section, we'll concern ourselves with the basic strategies of blackjack together with a card counting method to take advantage of the computer studies already done. Knowing these strategies and knowing how to count cards will make any blackjack player a winner. Before we go into this, we'll discuss the basic rules of blackjack and how it is played in a casino.

Rules of Play

Blackjack is played in casinos either as a one-deck, two-deck, or four-deck game. The more decks used by the house, the more the house has an advantage over the player and the more difficult it is for the average player to keep track of the cards and get an accurate count.

However, there are many casinos that still feature single-deck games, and the beginning player should play in those casinos. The method of play outlined here will deal with a single-deck game.

The standard 52-card deck is used, without the jokers. The 10, jack, queen, and king all have a value equal to 10. The ace can be used as either a 1 or 11, at the player's discretion. All other cards are equal to the value of their spots. A five is equal to 5 points, an eight to 8 points, and so on.

Any combination of a 10 value card (10, jack, queen, and king) and an ace is a blackjack, and this term gives the game its name. Whenever you are dealt a blackjack, you turn over your cards for an immediate win and are paid off at 3–2 by the dealer. You can only have a blackjack if you are given the ace together with the 10 value card on the first two cards initially dealt by the dealer.

The object of the game is to beat the dealer by having a higher total than he has. However, should the total of the cards in the hand exceed 21, then the hand is dead and is a loser. The player or dealer holding such a hand is said to have "busted." For example, if you are originally dealt 6 and 10, you have a total of 16. If you request another card, hoping to improve your hand and get as close to 21 as possible and are now dealt an 8, you have 24, and thus your hand totals over 21. You lose immediately. Your cards and chips are taken away from you.

One of the most important considerations in blackjack is when to ask for an additional card if that card will "bust" your hand. This is one of the basic strategies to be covered and will be dealt with thoroughly later in this chapter.

So far you know the value of the cards, know what constitutes a blackjack, and know what a "bust" means. I will now discuss the ace. It was mentioned earlier that an ace can be counted as either a 1 or an 11 at the player's discretion. Here's how that works.

If you are dealt a 10 value card and an ace, you automatically use the ace as an 11, so that you can turn over your blackjack and be paid off at 3–2. If, however, the other card dealt with the ace is not a 10 value card, then you may use your discretion and use the ace either as a 1 or an 11. For example, if you are dealt a 9 with the ace, you would want to count the ace as an 11, since you would then have a total of 20, a very high and usually winning total. However, if you are dealt a 5 with the ace, you would want to count the ace as 1, for a 6 total now. If you counted the ace as an 11, your ace, 5 would be considered a "soft 16," since you cannot now bust with a soft total. Let's see why.

After getting the ace and the 5, you request another card. Suppose you now get an 8. If you had counted the ace as 11, you would now have a total of 24, or a bust hand. But since you have the option of counting the ace as 1, your hand only totals 14 or 1+5+8. You can take another card if you wish, or you can stand pat, but you haven't busted.

With any soft totals (where the ace is counted as 11) you

can take another card with impunity if you wish, for you cannot bust your hand. If you hold ace, 6 for a soft 17 and take a card, no matter what card you take, you cannot go over 21. Even if you get a 10, your hand total will now be 1+6+10 for a 17. You have changed the value of the ace in your hand from 11 to 1, at your discretion. The concept of the ace as either 1 or 11 adds flavor and variety to this game, and in the charts later on, we'll show how to play soft totals.

The Deal

For purposes of this chapter, imagine that you're playing in a Strip hotel-casino in Las Vegas, in a single-deck game, using Las Vegas rules. The dealer, who is an employee of the casino, always plays against the players. Your object is to beat the dealer, not the other players; and in order to beat the dealer, you need a higher total than the dealer, or the dealer must bust. If you and dealer tie in number of points below the bust limit, the hand is a standoff, and no one pays or collects. If you have a higher total than the dealer or the dealer busts, you are paid off. If you have a lower total than the dealer, or have busted, the dealer wins and collects your chips.

All bets must be made prior to play. The average blackjack table has seats for five or six players, and in front of each seat is a betting box drawn on the layout. You bet by placing your chips in that box. You and the other players remain seated during the game, while the dealer stands facing the players across the table.

First, the dealer shuffles up the pack of cards, and then gives them to any player to cut. After they are cut, he squares the pack, then removes the first card from the top of the deck and places it either face up at the bottom of the pack or puts it aside in a plastic box, out of play. This is known as "burning the card" and has no other relevance except to put one card, the top card, out of play. Perhaps it is a tradition from the old days of gambling, preventing a dealer from stacking the deck, knowing the first card and dealing it to an accomplice.

After the first card is burned, the dealer begins his deal, giving the first player, the one to his left as he faces the players, a card dealt face down. He deals one card at a time in this clockwise fashion to all the players at the table and then deals himself a card face down. Then each player gets another card face down, and the dealer deals the final card to himself face up. All the players now have two cards face down, while the dealer has one card face down and the other face up. The face-up card is known as the "upcard" in blackjack.

Although the players' cards are usually dealt face down, it doesn't really matter whether or not the dealer sees these cards, for he is bound by strict rules of play. In this casino he must draw to his own hands totaling 16 or less and stand on all hands totaling 17 or more, whether soft 17 or not. The term for drawing a card in blackjack is "hit," and when a player or dealer takes an additional card, he "hits" his hand, or "takes a hit." (In some casinos, dealers must hit soft 17s on their own hands.) Thus, if the dealer holds 10, 6 for a 16, he must hit it, even if he knows that all the players facing him have totals less than 16, and he could beat them by not hitting his own hand.

In casino blackjack, the dealer has no options. He is bound by rigid rules from which he cannot deviate. All the options of blackjack remain with the players, and if they make good use of their options, they can have an advantage over the dealer.

Play of the Hand

Starting with the first player, the player to the dealer's left facing him, each player now plays his or her hand by either drawing one or more cards or standing pat.

The first player to receive cards or play out the hand is known in blackjack parlance as the "first baseman," and the last player to play out the hand is known as the "third baseman" or "anchor man."

You must turn over your cards in certain situations. First, if you are dealt an immediate blackjack, in which case you show it and are paid off at 3–2 on your bet. The second instance is where you have hit your hand and gone over the total of 21, or busted, in which case you turn over your cards, while the dealer removes both the cards and your chips.

If you want to double down, that is, double your bet and get an additional card, you also turn over your cards, showing them face up, announce that you are doubling down, and double your bet. If you want to split identical cards, you turn your cards face up, separate them and put down another bet identical to your original bet, for you now play two hands at once.

If you want to stand pat with your hand, you shove the cards under your chips, and that signifies that you don't want a hit, or, if you have already hit, shows that you don't want any more cards. If you do want a hit, you scrape the cards on the felt surface, brushing them toward you and get a card with this signal. This is done because of the noise in a casino, where it is often difficult to hear what a player is saying and the words or directions might be misinterpreted. That's why the scraping of cards for a hit is an almost universal practice where the cards are dealt face down.

Whether you stand or hit, whether or not you double down or split your cards is determined to a great extent by the rules of play at any particular casino and by the dealer's upcard. This will be discussed later in the section on basic strategies.

Let's follow the play of five players at an imaginary game in this Strip casino. All have already been dealt two cards face down and the dealer's upcard is a 7.

Player (1). He holds an ace, 9 for a 20. He stands pat by shoving his cards under his chips.

Player (2). He holds 10, 5 for a total of 15. He scrapes his cards for a hit and gets a jack. His total is now over 21 and he has busted; so he turns over his cards. His cards and his chips are taken away by the dealer, and his hand is now dead. Even if the dealer busts later on, the player can no longer win. He is out of the game at this point.

Player (3). He holds ace, queen for a blackjack. He turns over his cards immediately and is paid 3–2 for his bet, and his cards are taken away.

Player (4). She holds ace, 6 for a soft 17. She scrapes for a hit, since she cannot bust with a soft total, and gets a 3 for a total of 20. Now she stands by shoving her cards under her chips.

Player (5). He holds 2, 4 for a 6. He hits and gets an 8 for 14. He hits again and gets a 10 and busts. His cards and chips are taken away.

Now that all the players have played their hands, it is the dealer's turn. He turns over his hole card, which is a 4, and with his 7 upcard, he has a total of 11. Since he is the dealer, he has no options and cannot double down, so by the rules of the game, he must hit, since his total is less than 17. He deals himself a 6 for a total of 17, and now must stand. Both Player 1 and Player 4, who have totals of 20, beat him, and he pays them off.

All the cards that have been played in this round are now put either at the bottom of the deck behind the burned card or put into a plastic box to one side on top of the burned card; and the dealer now deals out a second round of cards from the same deck. Before he does this, all the players must make their bets.

Player's Options

We have been writing about player's options throughout this section, and now we'll state them fully.

- You can stand on any total and hit any total below 21. You are not bound by rigid rules of play as the dealer is. If you wish to stand on less than 17 you may do so, and if you wish to hit hands totaling more than 17 (usually soft hands) you may do so also.
- You may double down, that is, double your bet in certain instances. For example, if you hold a 6, 5 for a total of 11, you may wish to double your bet, for if you are dealt a 10 value card now, you will have 21 and cannot lose. You double down by turning over the first two cards dealt to you and placing an identical bet on the layout. If your original bet is $10, you put down $10 worth of chips next to your bet. Now you have a $20 bet working on that hand.

Doubling down is a definite advantage to the player, and the rules for doubling down vary from casino to casino and gambling region to gambling region. In Las Vegas, you may double down on any of the first two cards dealt to you, regardless of their total. At most casinos in northern Nevada, you may double down only on totals of 10 or 11 dealt on the first two cards.

After you make your double down bet, you are given only one additional card, usually dealt face down. You cannot draw or hit again in double down situations and are limited to that one card.

- Splitting pairs. You may split two identical cards such

an 8, 8 or 2, 2 or 10 value cards, such as jack, 10 (all 10 value cards are considered identical cards of the same rank in terms of splitting).

You do this by turning over the identically ranked cards, separating them, and making an identical bet next to the second card. You now play each hand separately. For instance, if you split 8s, you play the first 8. Let's say you hit and get a 10 for a total of 18. You stand and now play the second 8. If you get a 4 for a 12, you can now hit or stand at your option.

If you split aces, you get only one additional card on each ace. On all other splits, you may hit as often as you wish.

• You may take insurance if the dealer shows an ace as his upcard. This term, "insurance," is really a misnomer. What really is involved is that you are betting that the dealer has a blackjack, and if the dealer has a blackjack, he pays off the insurance bet. If the dealer doesn't have a blackjack, you lose your insurance bet.

You can only bet one-half of your original bet on this insurance bet. Here's how it works. The dealer's upcard is an ace. You have a $10 bet on your own hand, and the dealer asks if anyone wants "insurance." You bet $5 as your insurance bet (one-half your original bet) by placing the chips in front of your betting box. The dealer now peeks at his hole card. If he has a 10 value card there, he immediately turns it over, and pays off the insurance bet at 2–1, or $10; so, in reality, it is a standoff.

All the bets which were not insured are lost by the other players. If the dealer didn't have a blackjack, that is, a 10 value card in the hole, he wouldn't disclose his hole card, but would collect the losing insurance bets and continue the game as before, letting the players hit or stand on their cards.

If he does have a blackjack, he wins from all the players except those who made the insurance bet or those who have blackjacks themselves. If you have a blackjack and insure your bet, you are paid off at even money for your original bet. If you hadn't insured your blackjack, it is a standoff, a tie, and you collect nothing for your blackjack.

A dealer must peek at his hole card when he has an ace or a 10 value card showing as his upcard, to ascertain whether or not he has a blackjack. If he has a 10 value card showing, however, there is no provision for the players to insure a blackjack, which is just as well, since the odds are prohibitive against the dealer having a blackjack under those conditions.

Correct Basic Strategy

Basic strategy is governed by two considerations. First, by the upcard of the dealer, which is the only clue you have as to the potential value of the dealer's hand, and second, by the fact that the dealer is bound by predetermined rules and cannot deviate from them. He must hit all hands containing less than 17 and stand on all hands of 17 or above.

In all situations, the first option you have in basic strategy is hitting or standing. We'll mark a hitting hand as H and a standing hand as S in our first table.

For purposes of this strategy, all hands will be hard hands; that is, where the ace is counted as 1, or where there is no ace. A 10, 5 hand is a hard 15, whereas an ace, 4 hand is a soft 15. But a 10, 4, ace hand is a hard 15 also, for the ace must be considered as a 1 here, otherwise the hand would bust.

Player's Hand (Hard Totals)	Dealer's Upcard	Decision
12	2	H
12	3, 4, 5, 6	S
13, 14, 15, 16	2, 3, 4, 5, 6	S
12, 13, 14, 15, 16	7, 8, 9, 10, ace	H
17, 18, 19, 20	Any upcard	S

All hands below 12 are automatically hit because there is no way the player can bust. But first see doubling down strategy before making any decision on hands below 12.

SOFT HANDS

Since a player may double down in Vegas on any two cards, we'll include not only Hit and Stand but Double Down hands, which will be indicated by a D.

Player's Hand	Dealer's Upcard	Decision
A,2; A,3; A,4; A,5	2, 3, 7, 8, 9, 10, ace	H
A,2; A,3; A,4; A,5	4, 5, 6	D
A,6	2, 3, 4, 5, 6	D
A,7	2, 7, 8, ace	S
A,7	3, 4, 5, 6	D
A,7	9, 10	H
A,8; A,9	Any upcard	S

If casino rules don't permit doubling down on soft totals, then hit wherever doubling down is indicated, except for A, 7 against a 3, 4, 5, 6. In that case, stand.

SPLITTING PAIRS

Always split 8s and aces, and never split 4s, 5s, and 10s. The chart below shows splits on all other pairs. S stands for split.

Player's Hand	Dealer's Upcard	Decision
2s, 3s, and 6s	3, 4, 5, 6	S
7s	2, 3, 4, 5, 6	S
9s	2, 3, 4, 5, 6; 8, 9	S

Otherwise, don't split. For example, you won't split 6s against a dealer's upcard of 8 because its not on the chart.

DOUBLING DOWN STRATEGY— HARD TOTALS

Player's Hand	Dealer's Upcard	Decision
9	2, 3, 4, 5, 6	D
10	2, 3, 4, 5, 6, 7, 8, 9	D
11	Any upcard	D

DOUBLING DOWN STRATEGY—SOFT TOTALS

Player's Hand	Dealer's Upcard	Decision
A,2; A,3; A,4; A,5	4, 5, 6	D
A, 6	2, 3, 4, 5, 6	D
A, 7	3, 4, 5, 6	D

Never double down on hands below a hard 9 or on soft hands, other than those shown on the chart.

Counting Cards

After you've studied and mastered the basic strategies, and only then, should you learn to count cards. I'm going to present a simple method of counting, but as you improve it pays to study the more advanced methods of counting cards. Gambler's Book Club of Las Vegas, Nevada, Box 4115, Las Vegas, Nevada 89106 will be happy to send you its catalogue, which contains a complete section of blackjack books.

The counting method I'm going to outline is based on the sound and proven principle that the more small cards remaining in the deck in proportion to large cards, the more the deck is unfavorable to the player. This is so because the dealer is forced to hit all hands below 17, and if there are many small cards remaining in the deck, he'll make a great many of these hands by improving them. Conversely, the more large cards remaining in the deck in proportion to small cards, the more favorable the deck is to the player, since the dealer will bust on his weak hands.

Our method of counting is very simple. We'll count as all plus cards the 3, 4, 5, and 6 and as all minus cards the 10 value cards (10, jack, queen, and king). Other cards, including aces, are considered neutral and aren't included in the count and are to be disregarded for counting purposes. This count, though simple, is a powerful one, and can be used to win at blackjack in gambling casinos.

When a deck has a plus count, that is, when more small cards have been played than the 10 value cards, the deck is favorable for the player. When the deck is minus, more 10 value cards have been removed in proportion to the smaller cards, and the deck is unfavorable for the player.

Let's follow a round of play to see how this works. We'll study one hand at a time and keep a running count.

		Running Count—The deck is now
First Player	10, jack	–2
Second Player	6, 5, 10	–1
Third Player	king, 4	–1
Fourth Player	3, 5, 3, 9	+2
Fifth Player	10, 4, 6	+3

After this first round of play is over, the deck is now +3, or favorable for the player. We will take advantage of this favorable situation by raising our bets for the next round of play, since the advantage is with the players.

Tied up with the count is a betting strategy, with our bets determined by the count.

Opening round or neutral deck	2 units
Deck is plus 1 or plus 2	3 units
Deck is plus 3 or plus 4	4 units
Deck is plus 5 or more	5 units
Deck is minus any amount	1 unit

We never bet more than 5 units because we don't want to alert the casino personnel to the fact that we're altering our bets through a counting method. The whole principle we're following is a simple one—we raise our bets when the deck is favorable to us and lower it when the deck is unfavorable to the players.

The units bet can be any amount, ranging from $1 to $100. No matter what units you bet, this method will work and make money for you in the long run.

Also remember that the more cards dealt from the deck, the more powerful a plus reading is. Thus, a plus 2 deck after forty cards have been dealt is much stronger than a plus 2 deck after only six cards have been dealt. And aces are important to count, but all this can wait till you have mastered this basic counting and betting strategy. After you have it cold, move on to other more sophisticated counting methods.

This counting method is based only on single deck play. Take insurance when the deck is plus 3 or more, and only then.

Practice both the basic strategies and the count at home and learn them thoroughly. Master them. Once you have memorized them and *know every move* and can correctly make every play at home, and only then, go to a casino and bet real money.

After a while, you'll pick up shortcuts in counting. If you see king, jack, 4, 3, you'll see that the two pairs of minus and plus cards balance off and the deck is even, neither minus nor plus.

Blackjack is a game that can be beaten. To beat it, you must know the basic strategies, learn how to count, and then alter your bets accordingly. Once you start winning, the next thing you'll want to do is to play unhampered, without any heat from the casino personnel, so don't bet wildly, going from one unit to ten units when the deck is very favorable. You'll find that this chapter will give you a big edge, and don't spoil it by being barred from a casino.

VIII. POKER

Poker is the most popular of the gambling card games, for it is widely played in private homes as well as in poker clubs and casinos. There are many forms and variations of poker and it would take a book, not just a chapter, to cover them all. What we'll discuss here are basic principles of play applicable to all variations of poker.

First of all, poker is a game of skill; and though there is an element of luck involved, in the long run the skillful player will have a decided advantage over the weak or unskilled player. Poker is a game where a few strong players feed off the weak ones and make a good living in the process. Here are some of the principles you should follow, which will give you a decided edge in any poker game you enter.

• Don't be a jack-of-all-trades in poker. Learn a particular game, such as high draw, seven-card stud, or Hold 'Em, and stick to it. Study that game thoroughly and become an expert in that one game alone. Learn it well enough so that every move you make will be correct in terms of percentage and strategy.

If you don't become an expert in a particular game of poker so that your skill will prevail, don't play the game for serious money.

• Play at a betting level where your skill makes you the best player in the game or at least equal to the best. Often one or two players win money from all the other players. By being the best, you'll be a winner; not a contributor and loser.

A good way to know whether you're the best is to play in small stake games at the outset of your poker career. For example, if your game is seven-card stud, a game you've studied carefully and feel you've mastered, get your feet wet by playing in a small game, a $1 to $2 game. *If you can't win at this game, don't go into a bigger game.* And if you lose, don't blame luck or the run of the cards. It may be possible for the best player to lose in one session in any poker game but highly unlikely that he will be a constant loser against players below him in strength. I've interviewed some of the best players in the world and they rarely lose twice in succession, even against top fields.

So first find the correct level of your game. If you are an easy winner in a $1 to $2 game, move up to a $3 to $6 game, then a $5 to $10 game, and keep moving up as long as you win. Don't go into bigger stake games unless you can absolutely beat the players in the lower categories. This advice alone should save you a lot of money.

The higher the stakes, the tougher the competition, and when you move up to $20 minimum games, you're already encountering some tough players because this game can yield a win of several thousand dollars for a few nights' play. The majority of the big-money players are tough, but they're not impossible to beat, especially if you have the edge in skill and psychology.

If you find that you've beaten the $20 minimum games

and move higher and finally feel that you can beat any *limit* game, then you're perhaps ready for the no-limit games. I say perhaps because there are completely different strategies involved in no-limit games, dealing with the use of money and the ability to be very bold and aggressive. But it should be enough for the time being to get into high limit games, for you can make a bundle in those games. Several of the top players in the world prefer limit games to no-limit games, for they're better suited temperamentally for limit games.

• Learn the basic strategies, which are of the utmost importance. Among these are the following:

a. Stay in the game only with cards that can win for you. No matter how beautiful your cards look, if they're second best, all things considered, you're going to lose the pot to the best cards. This is true in most limit games, where it is more difficult to bluff with poorer cards. So if you have a pair of kings and another player is showing a pair of aces, get out. The odds are strongly in his favor and there's little chance of beating him. Don't chase winners, let losers chase you.

b. Learn the percentages in poker and play according to them. If the chances of drawing to a four-flush or four-straight is approximately 4.5–1, make sure that you're getting value for your money by having at least that much in the pot for every dollar you invest. Don't play for a flush with a four-flush when your bet will only net you 2–1 or 3–1. That's bad poker because you're ignoring the percentages. The losers play these hands all the time. Losers are eternal optimists; winners are realists.

c. If you have the best hand, make the others pay heavily for the privilege of trying to beat you. Sometimes, however, it pays to disguise or slow play such a hand; but generally, if you're a heavy favorite to win, make the opponents pay dearly for the chance to try and draw to beat you.

In the long run, you'll win with your strong hand over the opponent's four-flush many more times than he'll beat you.

Theoretically, about once every six hands he'll get his flush; but in the other pots, if you punish him with big bets, he'll be paying out a fortune to you.

d. Always remember that the money in the pot doesn't belong to you but will eventually belong to the winner of the pot. So no matter what you've put into the pot, if it is apparent that you won't win with your cards, fold your hand. *Don't throw good money after bad.* Never do that. That's the loser's way of playing. If you're beaten on board, its no crime or test of courage to give up on your hand. It's simply good poker, and you must respect and abide by the intelligent principles of play.

• Play an aggressive game. The best players in the world all have one thing in common. They are aggressive and the other players fear this aggression. Come out smoking, and play boldly when you have the goods. By constantly raising, you will make the other players fear you, and better still, you will disorient and disorganize their game. After a big raise by you, they won't know what to think. With constant aggression, they'll be unable to "read" or guess what you're holding. They'll have to respect every bet, and many times you'll win simply by aggressive play.

For example, suppose you remain in the pot to the last card in a game of seven-card stud, and your hand shows an open pair of tens, while your opponent has a nondescript hand showing a pair of nines. He hasn't been betting strongly with his cards, and now you're high on board, and its your turn to bet. All the cards have been dealt. The average player will probably check, pray the opponent checks also, and then hope to have the better hand. The strong player will bet the limit now, for he will think to himself, "by betting the limit, the odds are in my favor by 2–1. First, I may win this pot because he's afraid to call my bet; and second, if he does call, I may still have the best hand."

Not many people play that way, but not many poker

players are winners. So be aggressive and make the others fear you. In this way you'll have control over most of the poker games you enter.

• Study your opponents. This is of prime importance, for poker is not only a game of skill, but a game of psychological insight as well. That's what makes it the fascinating game it is. Psychology can be used at all levels of play, but the bigger the stakes, the more psychology plays a part. It's going to be hard to drive out an opponent when all he has to do is bet $5 to see your bet or raise; but when the stakes are in the hundreds or higher, then he'll really be in a bind.

All the top players have the ability to "read" the opponents, that is, to understand what hand they're holding, or as they say, "to put them on a hand." The best players are not so much concerned about their own cards; what they want to know is what the opponents are holding. Great players are very good at this, for they are constantly studying opponents for "tells," or unconscious mannerisms that give away their hands.

Many players make one terrible mistake in poker. They play the exact opposite of how they think they should be playing, and believe, by doing this, they're disguising their cards. For example, if they have aces wired, they grudgingly throw in a bet. If they have nothing but junk, they slam down their bet aggressively. Players who do this might as well open up their cards, for the astute opponents know exactly what they're doing.

Others give away their hands by talking. I was in a seven-card stud game in Las Vegas a couple of years ago and remember how talk cost an opponent dearly. I was dealt three aces rolled up, and being high, I made a small bet, figuring that I would keep the others in the game by slow playing my hand, for I was almost certain that my cards would win. Three other players stayed with me until the sixth card, at which time my open cards were ace, 2, 4 and 4. Together with my hidden cards, the pair of aces, I held a full house. I wasn't high, however, for one of my opponents held a pair of jacks, 9 and 10, and he had been raising continuously. He bet the limit, I raised the limit, and the other two, caught in the middle, folded their cards.

My opponent, who was a man in his fifties and who had been a moderate winner that evening, looked over his cards and then looked at my cards after my raise. "Damn," he said, "it's getting harder and harder to fill in these straights." At this point I immediately knew that he wasn't going after a straight at all, but had either two pair or three of a kind. He reraised my bet, and I reraised. Again, he looked at my cards, and said, "If I get my straight, its going to be higher than your little bitty straight. And I have a five in the hole, remember." He raised the limit.

I called his raise at this point, and we waited for the last card to be dealt. He shuffled up his three hole cards, and peeked at them, then put them down. He was high man, and he bet, I raised.

"If I made that straight," he said, "I got a higher straight than you. Jack high beats five high, isn't that right, dealer?"

The dealer said nothing and waited. The older man now spoke up again. "What do you say we put in some real money?" he suggested. He now asked the dealer if the game was table stakes if only two players were left. The dealer said there was no limit on raising in that situation.

"How about $300?" my opponent said to me.

"You must have that straight," I said.

"If I didn't have it, I wouldn't be betting $300, would I?"

"Well," I said, "make your bet."

"Now, young man, you're not going to run scary legged on me, if I make that bet, are you, now? I might not have that straight. I might be bluffing."

He counted out $300 in chips and bet them. I called his bet and sat back for him to show his hand. He picked up his three hole cards and turned them over, one by one. First, he turned over the case ace, then a pair of 9s. He had a full house, nines over jacks.

"Now, your little old straight or aces up, they ain't worth shit, are they?" he said, grinning. But his grin faded fast as I showed my aces, all three of them. He took a deep breath, coughed, and then stood up. Without saying another word, he left the table.

His patter was a perfect example of what I warn against. I knew he didn't have a straight and wasn't going after a straight. If I had a small straight or two pairs, I would have conceded the pot to him and never called any of his raises. His talk about the straight revealed that he wasn't going after a straight. In this instance, I had better cards and buried him; but that kind of talk, trying to disguise a hand so blatantly, only leads to trouble. His patter was supposedly a cover, but instead it peeled off his cover.

• Bluffing is another important aspect of poker. Bluffing is betting aggressively when you don't have the best cards in the hope that your bet will frighten your opponent or opponents into conceding the pot, even though they have superior cards. Used correctly, it is a great tool; but it must be used sparingly and at the right time. When caught in a bluff, always show that you were caught, for when you later have top cards, the opponents will think you're again bluffing and contribute to your winning pot.

Here are the rules for correct bluffing:

a. Don't try to bluff in low-limit games, where other players won't hesitate to call for a small bet.

b. Don't bluff against unskilled players who are winning. Bad players don't respect any cards and are eternal optimists. They'll stay on with any hand, no matter how terrible, with the expectation of drawing a card that will help the hand. And generally speaking, bad players don't like to be bluffed out of a pot; so even if they have nothing, they're tempted to call that last bet to make sure you really have better cards.

c. You can bluff a bad player who's losing heavily and counting his few remaining chips. His whole attitude might have changed, for now he is waiting for that one monster hand to get even, and he may concede hands that are playable.

d. It is easier to bluff a good player, who will respect strong hands and who isn't interested in throwing away money just to make certain he wasn't bluffed. A good player who's losing heavily is the best player to bluff.

e. Think of your position at the table when bluffing. If you're betting last or behind a bettor whom you wish to bluff, that's a good spot to be in. But if your position is poor, if you're under the gun or in front of a player you're trying to bluff, he might sandbag you and raise your bet. If he's in front of you and has already bet, your big raise indicates that, although he has good cards, you don't fear them in the least, for you have better cards. If you're in front of him, you've opened yourself up with your bet, and he can now go after you using the same reasoning, putting you into the same bad position you attempted to put him into.

f. Use money as well as position in bluffing. If you're a big winner and you're bluffing against losers, you have a big edge. Your money alone can drive them out of the pot. This is especially important in big-ante games where players don't have solidly formed hands at the outset of play, and your constant raises at that point force them to drop their hands, giving you all the antes. You can then use these antes as future leverage against them later on in the game.

If you study and follow all these principles, you should be a winner at poker. Study the game and practice playing by yourself. Study not only the correct moves and strategies, but study yourself in front of a mirror. Make certain your mannerisms are the same in every situation. Don't let your opponents have any advantage over you by "reading" your gestures or studying any inadvertent "tells" on your part. By playing aggressively, you will make this even more difficult. Then go out and play the game for money, find your level of play, and start winning.

One final word about poker. In any card game where players handle the cards or where there may be players in collusion, you must be on the lookout for cheating; and the bigger the game, the more the possibility of cheating exists, for a lot of money can be at stake.

If you're in a private game, playing among strangers, be on your guard. If the game is big enough, its whole purpose may be to fleece you, with all the other participants sharing in the proceeds. This is not unheard of. If you are in a game among strangers, be supercautious. If you're playing in a private game among friends, then still be cautious if the game is for large enough stakes. It requires some skill to be a card mechanic, but that skill is available to a lot of people.

In the casino games, a dealer handles the cards continually, and it is not likely that he is cheating, but players at the table may be in partnerships, helping one another out. In card clubs, each player handles and deals the cards, and so you must watch them carefully. This is not to say that you must be paranoid, but caution and alertness can't hurt you.

One of the easiest ways to be cheated is by collusion among other players, either in a private, casino, or club game. Players can work as silent partners and often do, and there is no way you're going to know this. If you find when you're in big pots with a particular player that another player also is in continually, raising and reraising, you may be set up as a sucker.

Also, when playing, keep your cards to yourself. The man next to you who has dropped out of the game and is peeking at your cards may be signaling them to a partner. Be alert and careful. There are a lot of cheats out in the world and many of them are attracted to poker games, where their cheating will be unobserved except by very discerning players, and where they can pick up a lot of money. So, my final word—keep your eyes open. Don't be cheated out of your winnings.

IX. BETTING ON SPORTS EVENTS

A tremendous amount of money is bet each year on the three major American sports: football, baseball, and basketball. Most of this betting is done illegally, for only Nevada has legal bookmakers; but the illegality of the system doesn't prevent literally millions of people from getting action on these sports. Baseball betting is done on major league teams, while football and basketball wagering is carried out on both professional and college teams.

During the season of any particular sport, most major city newspapers carry the *official line,* giving either the odds or point spreads on a variety of games. During the football season, all college games are played on Saturday with a few Friday night exceptions; and all pro games are played on Sunday and Monday nights (again, there are a few exceptions during the season). By Tuesday or Wednesday, there is an official betting line, usually originating out of Las Vegas, on most of the major college games and on all the pro games, naming the favorites and the point spread.

Baseball and basketball are played every day of the week in their seasons, and in most cases there are daily lines on these sports. These lines are published not only in Nevada but all over the country; and obviously are there because people are interested in knowing what the odds or point spreads are. Thousands of people around the country use these lines as a basis for making bets with illegal bookmakers. It is an immense hidden industry in America, running into the millions of dollars, and perhaps more.

How do you bet on sports events? Well, first you must know of a bookmaker or live in or near Nevada. Bets made in Nevada must be made in person and cannot be made by phone from either intrastate or interstate connections, for the casinos are very leery about breaking federal and state laws. However, your neighborhood bookmaker is much more friendly, and if he knows you, he'll not only take action over the phone but extend credit as well. In Nevada, on the other hand, it's all a cash business, with no credit allowed.

After you've found someone to take your bet, you must understand how to read the line for the particular sport you are betting on. Basketball and football are similar, in that a "point spread" is used, and one team will be so many points favorite over another team. A typical football day in the pros might look like this. The home teams are in capitals:

Favorite	**Point Spread**	**Underdog**
VIKINGS	6½	Bears
RAMS	10	49ers
Dolphins	17	GIANTS
Browns	½	LIONS
RAIDERS	20	Oilers
PATRIOTS	12½	Eagles

If you want to bet on the Vikings, you lay 6½ points. The extra half point assures the bookmaker that the game will not end in a tie as far as the point spread is concerned. Thus, if you bet on the Vikings, they must win by 7 points or more for you to win your bet. If they win by less than 7 points, you lose your bet. It won't matter that they won; as far as you're concerned, to win your bet, they must not only win but win "by the points."

The Rams, in our line, are 10 point favorites over the 49ers. Should you bet either side and the score ends up 20–10 in favor of the Rams, then the bet is a standoff, because, even though the Rams won the game, they didn't win or lose by the points. They simply tied.

If you bet an underdog, let's say the Eagles against the Patriots, you don't care if the Eagles lose, just so long as they lose by less than 13 points. If the Patriots won the game 24–12, you'd be happy if you bet on the Eagles, because the Patriots only won by 12 and didn't "cover the points." Having been given 12½ points, you'd win your bet.

So in reality, on any Saturday or Sunday afternoon during football season, there are two sets of games going on. There are the regular games, where the team scoring the most points wins, and then there are the same games from a bettor's viewpoint, where the only way for a team to really win is to beat the point spread.

If Notre Dame is favored over Purdue by 8 and wins 21–14, those who bet on Notre Dame are losers, while Notre Dame's fans, who didn't bet the game, are quite happy with the result. For the gambler, the team has to win by those points, not just win. That's why it's such a joke to gamblers to read sportscasters and writers who merely forecast the winner of a particular game and gloat when that team wins.

Anyone can do that. It's easy. If Ohio State is playing Indiana at Ohio State's football field in Columbus, any fool can predict that Ohio State will win. But the important question to the bettors is can the Buckeyes beat the spread?

Can they win by the points? If there were no points involved, this game would then be a simple bet. Bet on Ohio State. Beg borrow or steal, but get those bucks down on Ohio State. But the bookmakers don't make it that easy for the gambler; for if they favor Ohio State by 32 points, now we have a different situation. Can Ohio State roll up that many points? Do they have the incentive? Are they pointing for this game? What about the weather? A thousand considerations enter into the picture, and the gambler, weighing all these factors, is nothing but bemused when a sportscaster announces, "I pick Ohio State to trounce Indiana tomorrow in Columbus."

During basketball season, there are two lines, just as in football, one for the college teams and one for the pro game. Again, the point spread is the important consideration for bettors, and when bettors attend games, you can hear them shouting for points.

If the New York Knicks are playing the Boston Celtics in Boston Garden and the Celtics are 8 point favorites, if you're at the game, you'd be surprised to hear wild screams and shouts of "shoot, shoot" if the Celtics are holding onto a 6 point lead with thirty seconds left, passing the ball around and trying to kill the clock. Although most of the fans at the game will be content with a Celtics victory, the gamblers know that they'll lose unless 2 more points are scored by the Boston team. Two points will give them a tie, or push, while three will give them a victory. So, mingled with screams of "shoot" are cries of "foul, get a foul," for a three point play wins for the bettors on Boston.

It's much more interesting to watch sports events knowing the point spread, for then the entire perspective of the game changes. Because some owners of football teams are big bettors, there have been some strange scores and last minute moves by their teams that seemed incomprehensible to the TV or stadium audience. Spectators, of course, would have no way of knowing that team A, already leading by three points, was driving for a touchdown with forty seconds to play, rather than either running out the clock or taking a last second field goal, because the owner had a huge bet on team A and had given 7 points; a field goal wasn't enough to win his bet for him. Yes, strange things like that happen. Not often, but they happen.

Baseball, unlike football and basketball, is not bet by the points. The main reason for this is that baseball is a slower game with low scores, and many games are won or lost by one or two runs. Therefore, baseball is bet strictly by odds, with one team favored over the other. A typical baseball line in a newspaper might look like this, with the home team in capitals:

American League

Favorite	**Odds**	**Underdog**
NEW YORK	7½–8½	Cleveland
DETROIT	5½–6½	Chicago
Boston	6½–7½	OAKLAND
MILWAUKEE	Even–6	Minnesota

All of the odds relate to 5. Therefore, when 7½–8½ is quoted on the New York–Cleveland game, it is the shortened version of 7½–5, 8½–5. What this means is that New York is the favorite, and if you bet on the Yankees with the bookmaker, you must give 8½–5 odds. If you bet on Cleveland with the bookmaker, you receive only 7½–5. The difference is the vigorish or edge the bookmaker has on baseball bets. The Milwaukee–Minnesota game is quoted at Even–6, which means that if you bet on the favorite, Milwaukee, you must give the bookmaker 6–5, but if you bet on the underdog, Minnesota, you will get only even money on the game.

In addition to the standard point spread or odds bets, there are three other common bets one can make on sporting events. They are over and under bets, teasers, and parlays.

When you make an over or under bet, you are either betting that the combined total of runs or points by both teams will be over a certain designated number selected by the oddsmakers (over bet) or below a certain designated number (under bet). Here's how it works. Let's say that a particular baseball game has the designated number of runs fixed by the bookmaker at 9. If you think the two teams will score more than that number of runs, you make an "over" bet.

If you should believe that the two teams will score less than that number of runs, your bet will be an "under" bet. If you make either bet and the teams score the exact number of runs designated by the oddsmaker, then the bet is a standoff. On this kind of bet, the odds that you must lay are 11–10 with the bookmaker, who thus has his "vig" or edge no matter which way you bet.

Teasers are another common type of bet often resorted to by gamblers. Let's suppose that you want to bet on a particular pro football game. The Vikings are 10 point favorites over the Browns. At the same time you like the Eagles over the Giants, at 12 points. You can bet both games separately, giving the correct points, or you can ask the bookmaker for a "teaser" on both games. If you bet the teaser, he may allow you to give only 4½ points on the Viking game and 6½ on the Eagles game. Thus, you're saving 5½ points on each game, but in order to win the bet, both teams must win by the new teaser point spread. If one team wins and one team loses, you've lost both bets, for both bets are now tied together. If one team wins and the other ties by the points, it's a standoff. You won't win anything. If both tie, it's a standoff also. But remember, should either team lose by the points, you have a losing bet. Generally, on teaser bets, no "vig" is attached to the bets, because the bookmaker now has enough of an edge, since you have to pick two winners instead of one to win your teaser bet. However, points given and odds quoted vary depending upon the bookmaker and section of the country.

When you make parlay bets, you're betting on two or more games at one time without teasers. One bet covers all the games, and the odds you'll receive vary from bookmaker to bookmaker and sports parlor to sports parlor. At one of the largest sports books in Las Vegas, if you bet a two game parlay in basketball, you receive 11–5 for your bet. Since the correct odds are 3–1, it's an extremely bad bet and gets worse the more games you bet.

For example, a three team parlay pays 5–1, when the correct odds are 7–1. The situation at this casino is a little better for basketball for some reason, where a two team parlay pays 13–5 instead of the correct 3–1, and a three team parlay pays 6–1 instead of 7–1. In any event, you're giving too much to the house, and my advice is never to bet parlays or parlay cards. They're strictly for suckers.

In basketball and football betting, where no odds are laid, where everything is based on the point spread, the typical bet is made at 11–10 in the bookmaker's favor. This means that you must lay $11 as your bet, and you'll lose the $11 if you lose the bet, but the bookmaker will only pay you $10 if you win your bet. Bets in multiples of $10 are paid off in the same way. If you want $100 worth of action on a football or basketball bet, you must lay $110–$100. The difference is the "vig" or advantage that the bookmaker has over the bettor.

This advantage boils down to 4.76 percent when betting on basketball and football games. The advantage is slightly different in figuring baseball betting. On the average 20-Cent Line, where the odds are listed as 6–7, and 7½–8½, each bet is calculated separately. For example, if you bet the favorite when the odds are 6–7, and thus are giving 7–5, when the true odds are 6½–5, the bookmaker has an edge of 3.11 percent. But, if you bet the underdog and take 6–5 instead of the true 6½–5, the bookmaker has an edge of 4.35 percent. On a 7½–8½ line, if you bet the favorite and get 7½–5 instead of 8–5, the bookmaker's advantage is 2.26 percent, and if you bet the underdog and receive 7½–5 instead of the true odds of 8–5, the vig is now up to 3.85 percent. As can be readily seen, the bettor who takes the favorite gets better odds, and the higher the spread, the better the odds. For example, 8–9 odds are much better for the player than 6–7.

Can you make money betting on sports events? The answer is a qualified yes, for although the bookmaker's advantage is higher than the house edge in casino games, it is much lower than in horse racing. There are limited places where bets can be made on casino games, but sports betting is prevalent around the country; and it is the only kind of betting many players do. Therefore, I have devoted a great deal of space to sports betting; and I believe, with a careful study of the factors that make one a winner betting on sports events, together with proper money management, the bettor can overcome the slight edge the bookmaker has. We'll cover each sport individually in the next chapter.

X. HOW TO GAMBLE INTELLIGENTLY ON SPORTS EVENTS

There are general as well as specific rules that apply to each sport. First, let's state the general rules before going into the specifics. These rules must be followed in order to make money at sports betting.

- Practice at home by picking games in your particular sport, making imaginary bets. Keep a record of your wins and losses, and include the bookmaker's "vig" with your losses. Until you can make money at home without betting real money, don't make real bets. Not only must you win imaginary money, but you must win consistently, over a period of time.

The best way to practice is to create your own line before you see the official line. If the official line differs, then see how you would have done with your own forecast. Your own line will have to be more correct than the official line in order to make money. If you think team A should be 6 points over team B, and the official line has that game even, then make an imaginary bet on team A, and if you forecast correctly, you should win the bet.

• Put aside money for sports betting that you can afford to lose. Don't play with "scared" money and don't play with money that you need for essentials. The reason for this is simple. If you can afford to lose the money (which doesn't mean you will, of course) you'll be able to keep a clear head through temporary adversity, and with the tension involved in betting on games, you'll need that clear head to be a winner.

• Divide your total bankroll into twenty equal parts and don't bet more than one equal part or unit on any event at the outset. If you find that you're a consistent winner, you may now trust your judgment and make bigger bets on games that you feel the bookmakers have misread. When you find that the oddsmakers differ greatly with your line, and if you've had considerable and consistent success in these situations, then you might bet up to five units on these games. But never bet so much that two or three bets will wipe you out.

To beat the bookmaker you must win consistently, and if you can do this, there's no point in taking a chance with your total bankroll or a good part of it. Don't get greedy. If you're winning, don't change your pattern to try and make a killing. That's the way to sure losses.

• Above all, don't increase your bets when you're losing in order to break even. And don't make desperate "hunch" bets when you're losing. That's the surest way to go broke. That's the way the losers handle their money; don't be a loser. *Be a winner at all times in thought and action.* And in order to be a winner, you must make bets based on intelligent and clear thinking, not on hunches. The minute you decide to make a hunch bet, stop betting and save your money.

• Study the particular sport you want to bet on, and stick to that sport alone. If basketball and football season overlap and you've been winning consistently on football, stay with football. Don't make bets on a sport you haven't thoroughly studied, and don't make bets for action's sake alone. Football is played on weekends only, while basketball is played every day of the week. You had better learn self-control and stay away from basketball action if you have been winning at football and want to continue to be a winner. Reread the chapter on self-control whenever you feel weak and edgy for action.

• Specialize and then specialize again and again, till you're an expert on one conference or on a limited number of teams. If you're betting on college games, stick with a few teams in a couple of conferences and know all about these teams. Subscribe to the college and hometown newspapers if you're betting serious money, and get all the information you can. If you're betting the pros, then follow six or eight teams and know these teams thoroughly. Be able to spot overlays, situations in which the oddsmakers have misinterpreted the point spread. You'll be able to spot them because you should know more than the oddsmakers if you want to win money. *Knowledge is power*—never forget that.

• When you're betting seriously, throw out all attachments and sentimentality. If your alma mater is playing on national TV, don't make a bet on them just because you graduated from that school. You can enjoy the game without a bet. And don't bet on games when you're a fan of one particular club. Stop being a fan; be a realist. Betting sports events is a business, a serious business involving cold cash; always keep that in mind. Sentimentality doesn't and shouldn't mix with business. Don't let attachments rob you of the opportunity to make a lot of money.

• Don't make bets just because you need action. Avoid that kind of thinking; it's the way losers think. If you find no good bets that day or that weekend, lay off and don't bet. If a game is on TV and you can't figure out which side to bet on, keep your money in your pocket. Don't create action for excitement. If you do, you'll wind up a loser.

• Avoid parlays at all costs. They're sucker bets, and if you're a sucker, you can't be a winner. Forget about the enhanced odds; they're not good enough. And don't get sucked into bets that are exotic or that you don't understand fully in terms of odds or percentages. Occasionally you might want to make teaser bets when you feel certain that both teams are bad overlays in the first place. But don't make teaser bets if they'll affect your overall strategy. Your best bet is an individual wager on a particular game.

• If you find yourself losing real money after winning money on paper with imaginary bets and can't figure out what went wrong, the first thing you should do is stop betting. Then think out and examine your approach and strategy without making further bets. Don't make any decisions under pressure or while depressed or anxious. *Decisions made under these conditions are always destructive.* And destructive decisions are the most expensive of all decisions.

If you follow these ten rules, you're well on your way to winning. Now, let's deal with individual sports.

Baseball

Baseball is a sport that can give you action almost every day during its season; so you must be selective about your bets. Pick a limited number of teams to follow and know these teams as well as you can. If possible, subscribe to the hometown newspapers. Read the *Sporting News,* which is the bible of baseball news. Know what the home parks or stadiums of these teams are like. Because of wind factors or dimensions, some team parks favor right-handed hitters or pitchers. If the park favors a right-handed team, and a team composed mostly of southpaw players is coming in, this factor becomes very important in determining your bet. And some stadiums favor batters over pitchers and vice-versa. These factors are important in games and in determining "over and under" bets.

Get to know the strengths and weaknesses of the teams you follow, especially their pitching staffs. Pitching is the most important element of baseball, and when odds are determined on baseball games, the first factor the oddsmakers take into consideration is the pitchers for that game. A mediocre team with a great pitcher will be favored over a better team with a mediocre pitcher. Know all about the pitchers; their strengths and weaknesses. Know what their records are against other teams. Do this by keeping records for yourself. You should know not only the pitchers' past performance records against individual teams but how well they've been pitching recently.

When pitchers are well matched, then you must look to other factors, such as home park advantages and the relative strengths of the two teams. Stay with teams that are on winning streaks and are hot. Don't guess when a team will get hot; when it's winning, it's hot, and stick with that team.

And finally, pick teams that can win. Winning is the name of the game in baseball. Runs don't count; wins do. If a team can win by one run consistently, it's a better team to bet on than a hot and cold team that wins by five runs one day but loses by six the next time out.

Football

This sport is divided into two distinct areas: the college game and the pro game. First, let's examine the college game.

It's best when betting on football at the college level to stick to a couple of conferences, either those that you have a feel for or those that are in your section of the country, so that you will have access to the latest news concerning injuries, dissension, etc. If you live in Providence, Rhode Island, you're going to read a great deal about Brown University and the Ivy League. If you live in Detroit, you're going to be reading Big Ten news, and if you live in San Francisco, its all Pac 10.

Unless you can get good information about the Pac 10 in Providence, don't bet that conference. This is logical advice, but so many football bettors simply want action and make bets without thinking of consequences. They look in their Hartford paper and see that USC is 12 points over UCLA and say to themselves, "Hah, UCLA is a good bet," without the faintest notion of why UCLA is a 12 point underdog and then wake up the next day with another losing bet; and, reading the results of the game, they find out for the first time that two key linemen for UCLA were on the injured list and didn't play.

Get as much information as you can about the conferences you're going to follow and about the teams within the conference. Even if you follow a particular conference, bet on only a few of the teams in the conference that *you know better than the bookie or oddsmaker.* Having an edge on information will give you an edge in profits. The bookmakers and oddsmakers have hundreds of teams to make point spreads on, and their judgment may be way off at times, while you have five or six teams to follow, and your judgment, if objective and based on facts, should be superior to the oddsmakers.

Pick consistent teams within the conference, if possible. Teams that are hot one week and cold the next spell trouble. The stronger the team, the more steady it will be week after week. If you're betting the Big 8 conference, you might want to stick with Nebraska and Oklahoma rather than with Kansas State and Iowa State.

However, much more will be written about Oklahoma and Nebraska, not only locally but nationwide, than about the weaker sisters in the Big 8, so you may make weakness into strength by knowing all about Kansas State and Iowa State. If you find that betting on the obscure teams will make money for you, because they're not obscure to you, then work that method of winning. Do whatever is necessary and follow whatever teams will give you betting profits.

I personally know a bettor who made a good living betting on weak college teams like Bucknell and Colgate, week after week. He subscribed to the college and local newspapers, and the news about these teams was the big news in sports for these newspapers. Colgate and Bucknell played other small schools, schools that few bettors paid attention to, but he studied these games carefully. Bookmakers didn't always come up with the right lines on these games, for sometimes they'd post a line based simply on comparative won-lost records. This bettor knew much more than the bookmakers or oddsmakers did and put his knowledge to good use.

Another friend followed only one team, his alma mater, and made several thousand dollars betting the team one season. He not only subscribed to the hometown and college papers but regularly visited the campus as an alumnus, spoke to the players and coaching staff and watched the team workouts. He got to know the team and the coaches quite well and offered to be an unofficial scout for the team in his home district, not only to recruit players but to watch games by future opponents. In that way, he discussed each game in depth with the coaches and players, and he had inside information available only to a select few and certainly not to the bookmakers. He knew more about that team than *anyone* betting its games, and he really hurt the bookies that season.

That's the way to win, because, with the confidence your knowledge gives you, you can really make some big bets and punish the bookmakers when they've misstated the correct spread.

The next season my friend was tied down to his own business affairs and didn't have the same information available. He continued to bet on his team but had only a mediocre season and then quit betting. He was smart enough to know that if you don't have an edge over the bookie, you can't win, and thus you shouldn't bet.

In college football, there are many factors that are weighed for each game. Among these are comparative strengths of the two teams, the strength of their previous rivals, their won-lost record, and the home team advantage. What is not figured into the result, but is of prime importance, is the schedule. If Ohio State is going to play its great rival, Michigan, the next week, they might not want to risk injury against Iowa; and unless Ohio State is pushing for a Number 1 ranking in the nation, it might not roll up the score or try that hard.

If Michigan, on the other hand, is playing Purdue, and Purdue was the only conference team to beat them the previous season, Ohio State or no Ohio State, Purdue is going to be punished if Michigan can manage it.

Too many bettors of college football examine only the present season and disregard the past. The past is just as important. Teams that play each other year after year have long memories. Teams that have been humiliated in the past by another team and now are stronger will take out their revenge the year they have the better team. Look at the Notre Dame–Army scores during the Second World War, when suddenly, Army was on top of the football heap. All their past humiliations at the hands of Notre Dame were made up for by Army in those war years.

As you must look to the past, look to the future. Who is next on the schedule? Is this next game more important than the previous or present one, so that the team you like won't be up for the present game? Is the present game a conference game? Some teams do their best only for conference games; all other games are treated as incidental games.

National rankings are important. A team fighting for a high national ranking is generally going to roll up big scores against hapless rivals to impress the writers and coaches who make up the national rankings. Teams like Notre Dame and Alabama usually have weak schedules year after year, with several outclassed opponents included as "breathers." When these schools are going for the Number 1 spot in the nation, they have no mercy against the weak sisters. On the other hand, when they themselves have been beaten a couple of times during the season, they will play an easier game against poorer teams.

Know about and examine the important rivalries that exist between college teams. When Army plays Navy, you can sometimes throw away the comparative scores and records of these two teams. This is the big game that makes up for the whole season. Likewise, Harvard–Yale or Oklahoma–Texas or any number of other traditional rivalries. Some teams have not only one but a few key rivals. In those games, give the underdog most of your consideration. Anything can happen in big games played by traditional rivals.

What I've been suggesting is that you develop a psychological insight as well in dealing with college games. The bookies may take traditional rivalries into consideration when making the odds, but they might not take past humiliations and revenge factors into consideration, and these are very important in college football. Having this knowledge will give you a big advantage in betting certain games.

And finally, try a half-season or a whole season of betting on paper. See if your knowledge gives you an edge and makes you money on mind bets alone. If it doesn't, you're not ready to bet real money, or it may be that sports betting on college football is not for you. Don't put out cash till you can beat the game on paper.

Pro Football

Unlike college football, pro football these last few years has become a cut and dried game, with more and more coaches taking a very conservative approach. The games reflect this conservatism and most of the moves are predictable. Coaches are afraid to take chances. They always punt on fourth down; they run on first down; every move is cautious. As a result of this attitude college football tends to be more of an exciting and wide open game than pro football, and I believe it will be a matter of time before pro football will either have to change to a less static image or lose some of its immense popularity.

In pro football, the quarterback is king and is the key man in the offense, and subsequently, on the team. If a quarterback is injured, the point spread against that team changes radically. So the most important aspect of the game, all other things taken into consideration, is the quarterback, his effectiveness, health, and ability.

Of course, a quarterback alone can't make a team into a winner. The strengths of a pro team are usually divided up as follows: running game, passing game, offensive line, defensive line, linebackers, defensive secondary, defense against the rush and pass, and kicking game. Weighing all these factors, the oddsmakers get a preliminary line on the game.

In addition, the home field advantage is worth a couple of points and is an important consideration. However, the discerning bettor recognizes that the home field can be a disadvantage, particularly if the fans are down on a team or quarterback. In that case, the team or individual players may perform at a sub-par level before their disillusioned and angry fans.

In pro football, rivalries mean little because this is a game played by professional athletes and not rah-rah boys. What is important in matchups is not the rivalry but how well some teams do against other teams on a historic basis. Some teams have the hex over others, for some reason or other. This should always be taken into consideration, and past season records should be studied as well as the present season results.

Since players are traded often, a key player, such as a quarterback or middle linebacker, may play beyond his expected abilities against a team that traded him away or dumped him. However, since players expect to be traded, since this is part of the game, it doesn't mean automatically that a traded player will necessarily play well against his former teammates. But sometimes, if a player was handled badly by a previous team, he may go all out against that team.

Teams in pro ball get hot and go on big winning streaks. Stay with a hot team, and avoid teams that alter radically from week to week. Study the reports of the teams, looking for trouble spots, such as internal dissension, salary disputes, and coach-team problems. All of these factors are to be weighed, for a team that is racked by dissension, no matter how strong it appears on paper, tends to be weaker on the playing field.

Coaching is another important consideration. Some coaches, such as Don Schula and George Allen, are winning coaches and get the most out of ballplayers. Other coaches, no matter how affable, are duds when it comes to motivating their teams to victory. And a weak or mediocre coach can actually hurt his team. Stay with winning coaches.

In pro ball, because of the nationwide coverage given by magazines, TV, and newspapers you can follow several more teams than you can in college ball, and in studying the line, you will often see an overlay. Take advantage of incorrect lines and bet the games you feel have the mistaken point spreads. Sometimes a hidden factor, such as injury, will be present and affect the point spread, but this rarely occurs, since, in pro football, all injuries must be publicly reported in advance, and thus there are fewer surprises in pro football.

The best way to prepare for serious betting is to study the teams, using the suggestions I've outlined; and then before you look at the official line, *make your own line.* Then compare it to the official line, and then, after the Sunday results, look at the scores and see how well you did as an oddsmaker. If you're doing better than the bookmakers and can win consistently this way on paper, it's time to test the waters and make real money bets, based on your own line.

However, if your line is faulty, and you can't make money on paper, then avoid betting real cash. You may not be taking all factors into consideration or weighing them properly; and until you can beat pro football games regularly without betting money, don't bet money.

Basketball

In this sport you also have a college game and a pro game, both of which can be bet on. There are many more college basketball teams than football teams because a college team needs fewer players, a smaller auditorium or arena, and limited equipment. Since the basketball schedules cover as many as twenty-five games instead of football's ten or eleven games, there is much more action available, and the action is not restricted to Saturdays only.

You can get all the action you want betting on college basketball, but you have to be careful, for a multiplicity of bets can quickly deplete your bankroll, if you encounter a losing streak. In college basketball, you should be careful to specialize in a couple of conferences and several independent teams and to subscribe to college and local newspapers if possible to get as much information as you can about the players and coaches.

Not only the strength of the teams but the home court

advantage is of prime importance. Refereeing can alter a game considerably because of foul calls, and you must give much added weight to the home team because of this factor.

The other psychological factors, such as dissension in the club cannot be discounted, in this day when college stars are merely biding their time to make huge money in the pros. Study the coaches as well. Good coaches make a world of difference, and certain coaches have the ability to raise their teams to great heights, particularly in critical games.

Travel is more of a factor in basketball than in football, for there is constant movement by the teams, and some teams travel across the country continually. A team on the road can be a weary one, and thus you must always examine the schedules and take this into consideration, for a tired or exhausted team won't be able to play up to its usual strength.

Pro Basketball

The schedule in pro basketball is brutal, for, counting the playoffs, more than 120 games may be played between exhibitions, regular season, and post-season games, and this has a debilitating effect on any team. Thus, one of the factors to be considered is the conditioning of a team by a coach. Teams that are fast-break or running teams are generally in better condition than other teams and will not tire so easily.

Study the schedule carefully. A team that has a long road trip night after night will tire considerably, and on some nights it won't even try to win.

I recall going with a good friend to Madison Square Garden a few years ago for the preliminary workout of a visiting pro team, one of whose key members had been a fellow student of my friend's at college. My friend, whom I'll call Max, asked the pro star how he felt, and the player, who was a big forward, said "Man, I'm beat, just beat. We flew in just now from Chicago... been on the road for a week now."

Max and I left the Garden after purchasing tickets for the game that night, and Max said he was going to call his bookie and place a big bet on the game. I asked him who he was betting on, and he named his friend's team. I told him he was crazy... he had just been given a message.

"What message?" Max asked.

"He told you he was tired. He won't try tonight."

"Then he would have told me."

"No, he couldn't do that. But he gave you the same message in other words."

My friend bet on the visiting team. The Knicks were 5 point favorites that night against his friend's team, and I was tempted to bet a bundle on the Knicks, but I didn't want to go against my friend. Anyway, the Knicks won by 18 points and his friend's team looked as though they were standing still.

Home team advantage has become more and more important in the pro ranks these last few years. This past season home teams hardly lost any games in their own arenas, and this has caused a definite break in the balance of home-away games. You must take the home team, with home officiating, into consideration, and give it extra weight these days.

There's continual action in the pros, and if you follow a limited number of teams and know their schedules, their attitude, their abilities, and everything else you can know about them, you stand a very good chance of making money betting pro basketball. Be selective, and you should do well against the bookmakers.

XI. HORSE RACE BETTING

Betting on the horses, or the "ponies," as the racetrack enthusiasts call them, is one of the most popular of the American gambling sports, and millions of spectators attend racetracks throughout America, betting basically on three types of horse races. The most popular are those involving thoroughbred horses. These horses run in such famous stake races as the Kentucky Derby and Belmont Stakes.

The standardbreds are trained to run with a sulky behind them, rather than a jockey in their saddle, either as trotters or pacers, depending on the gait they use. Trotting races became very popular after the Second World War, and now these horses run at tracks throughout the country, usually in night racing.

Finally, there are the quarter horses, which are bred and trained to spurt or sprint for no more than a quarter of a mile; thus their name. This type of racing is getting more and more popular, especially in the Southwest and West, where quarter horses have a big following.

Watching horses run after making a bet on one of them can be very exciting, but unfortunately, the greed of the racetracks and the states where betting on horses is permitted, make it practically impossible for you to have any chance to win money. Between the taxes, the track take, and the breakage, you are facing a disadvantage of about 18 to 20 percent, which is extremely difficult to overcome. On top of that, you are charged an admission to the track, must pay for your own parking, and must even purchase a track program in addition to the *Racing Form*. By the time you are ready to bet the first race, you are already about $10 in the hole.

Then you must face the track edge. The total bet on each race is called the handle, and from each race, about 18 percent is deducted for taxes, etc. Slowly but surely, by the end of the day, a great deal of bettors' money is siphoned off, so that the only winners are the people who run the tracks and the tax collectors. The hapless horseplayers pay for all this.

If it wasn't for this horrendous situation, I would suggest a serious examination of possibilities to beat the races, but faced with an 18 percent track cut, there is no purpose to it.

I've never met a horseplayer who is ahead financially, and most of them die broke, trying to beat the races. That 18 percent just eats them up. The reason horse racing is still so popular is that it's an exciting sport to watch, and there are so many factors involved in picking winners that optimism reigns supreme. It seems so easy to pick a winner, theoretically. All one has to do is examine the *Racing Form* and look at the past performances of the horses in a race. Then the bettor examines the present conditions of the track and the race.

Some thoroughbreds are sprinters, others are better at longer distances. Some run best on dirt; others on grass. There are horses that can't carry more than a certain weight without slowing down. Horses run in different classes of races. The best horses run in "stake" races. Below them come handicap, allowance, and finally, the lowest category of race, the claiming race.

There are other factors to examine besides the horse itself and the race. Each horse must be ridden by a jockey, either in the saddle or in the sulky, and certain jockeys are more competent than others. In addition to these conditions, breeding plays a large role. Horses are bred for certain traits, and it's good to know who the sire and dam were (which is shown on the track program). If the sire was a sprinter, there's a good chance that the colt or filly in the race is also a sprinter. And where the best are bred to the best, it follows, at times, that the progeny are also class horses. Sometimes, but not always.

In addition to these factors, there is the aspect of the horse's present condition, its recent performances, and its training methods. Recent workouts are shown in the *Racing Form,* and this gives some indication of the horse's fitness to run that day. After you examine and digest all these facts you can turn to the selections of professional handicappers, the so-called experts, who list their choices for each race. And you may buy "tout sheets" of independent handicappers. Then you are ready to study the final factor: the money bet on each horse in the race.

All American tracks use a totalizer or "tote" system, whereby the odds are determined by the amount of money bet on each horse in each race, divided by the total handle of that race, minus the 18 to 20 percent skimmed off the top. Many bettors use the board odds as an indication of how well "the smart money" likes a horse. Smart money is money bet by the insiders, the big bettors at the track; and often, when these insiders know something, they wait until the last minute to sock down their bets. These last minute shifts in odds are closely followed by a number of bettors.

Some horseplayers can't handicap horses at all and go

along with the crowd, betting on favorites in every race. They feel if the public likes the horse, there must be a good reason to bet that horse, even though the public is wrong on the average, two-thirds of the time.

Whatever factors are followed, it is a tough game to beat. In the end, most bettors are buried by the track edge, that 18 to 20 percent that never varies and that is skimmed off in every race.

Perhaps there are some bettors who have beaten the races or feel they can do so. If you feel you can win by betting on horse races, I'd strongly advise you not to bet any real cash until you can win consistently theoretically, by imaginary bets. If you can't show a paper profit, don't go and bet your money at the track or with Off-Track betting parlors.

All the factors I've outlined could be taken into consideration, plus others, such as speed ratings, or any combination of these factors. But remember, it's awfully difficult to find anyone who's ahead at the races. And all the experts, the handicappers, show a loss on their selections over any period of time, and none shows a profit over a particular year. If they can't pick winners, with their access to private clockings and information from trainers and owners, who can pick winners?

Racing is a great spectacle and has endured for centuries. If no betting were allowed at the tracks, of course, despite the beauty of the horses, the flamboyance of the jockey's silks, and such, horse racing would fold up overnight. If you want a little excitement and occasionally feel that a day at the races is your price for entertainment, then by all means go to a nearby track. You can make small bets and scream your head off for the horse you bet on and have a good time. But for serious betting, for gambling to win, stay away from all kinds of racetracks.

My advice is the same for betting on greyhound races. The track and state exact their edge from these types of races, and it's suicide to overcome 18 percent race after race.

More and more states are opening Off-Track betting parlors (OTB) and there is often more action at the parlors themselves than at the tracks. But, in betting this way, you're facing more of a handicap, for you can't see the last minute changes in race odds, and one worthwhile tool, where the money is being bet, is lost to you.

So, my final advice is this—don't bet real money on horse races till you can absolutely and truthfully beat them on paper with imaginary money. But the edge is so tough that I'd suggest putting your energy into other methods of gambling; either on sports events or the casino games recommended in this book.

XII. PRIVATE GAMES

Under this category, we'll briefly discuss backgammon, several card games, and craps, played as a private game.

Backgammon

Backgammon is becoming more and more popular as a gambling game, and its combination of skill and luck, together with the doubling cube, make it an exciting betting game. My advice at backgammon is this—study the game carefully and thoroughly before you attempt to play it for stakes. Get to be as skillful as you can. Once you feel you've mastered its fine points, play for small stakes, and when you can *win steadily,* play for bigger money. As with most gambling games, the bigger the stakes, the more skillful the opposition. Don't play against better players, unless the stakes are small, and you want to upgrade your game.

There are some fine books on the subject, written by champions. Study the books, study the moves by yourself. Play against yourself when you're learning. Until you are sure of every opening move and the correct procedure for the other standard moves, and this becomes second nature to you, don't play for money. Be firmly in control of your game before you risk anything of value on it. Don't be impatient. Patience in learning is the mark of a winner.

Bridge

Bridge is often played for money, as well as for master points, and here again, there are various levels of skill involved. Don't play this game for big stakes unless you're an expert, because there are many fine bridge players around for whom bridge is a lifelong obsession. It's a good game to play for low stakes because of the skill involved. But if you're going to play for big money, be sure you're the best among the group playing. That's the philosophy of a good friend of mine who's a world class player. "Make sure you're the best at the table; otherwise don't play the game for serious money." It's very sound advice.

Private Card Games

In all other private card games played for serious stakes, such as blackjack, gin rummy, and pinochle, remember that you not only will be coming up against very tough players when you play for big money, but cheating is prevalent. Card sharps and mechanics can do things with a deck of cards that you wouldn't believe and that you wouldn't be aware of until they emptied your pockets.

Use the same skills outlined in the chapter on blackjack

for the private game, altering it to accommodate the different rules in the private game. If you can beat casino blackjack, you can have a ball at the private game, for it's been my experience that players in these games have no conception of correct basic strategy.

Gin rummy is a very popular gambling game, played either as a team game with two pairs of partners or as an individual match. It's a game of skill, and the strong player will prevail over the weak player in the long run.

Unless you can win for small stakes consistently, don't feel that you have the skill to play for bigger stakes. Gin, while not as complicated as bridge, is a game that must be mastered nevertheless; and in addition, you must train your card memory to learn which cards have already been played. A good test of how well you play is to try, near the end of any particular deal, to name every card in your opponent's hand: what lays he's holding and what odd cards he has as well. If you can't do this, you're going to have a lot of trouble playing against top-flight opposition for big stakes.

There are many other card games played for stakes, but in this book, we've basically concentrated on the most popular of the gambling card games and poker in particular.

If there's a particular card game you play for money, not covered here, follow the same rules I've outlined. Learn your game thoroughly; be as good as you can. Play for smaller stakes at the outset; when you're a consistent winner, go into the bigger games. Watch out for cheats. All this advice can do is help you become a winner, so follow it.

Craps—Private Game

We've thoroughly discussed casino or bank craps, but the private game is also a great gambling game and is played extensively. The few hints I'm going to give you now about gambling at craps are going to earn you a lot of money. The game is played basically the same way as casino craps, except that there are no come, place, field, or proposition bets. Everything is determined by the come-out roll, and, as you remember, a 7 or 11 wins for the right bettor; a 2, 3, or 12 (all called craps) loses, and all other numbers become points, which have to be repeated before the 7 comes up. For the wrong bettor, the whole procedure is reversed, except that, in the private game, the 12 isn't barred and is a winner for the wrong or don't player.

Having the 12 means that the wrong bettor, on every come-out roll, has an edge of about 1.4 percent. If the casino is satisfied with this edge, you should be also, so bet against the dice whenever you can. In private games, the wrong bettor also gets another bonus—although the odds against making a 4, 5, 9, or 10 are correct, in private games the 6 and 8 are often bet against at even-money odds. So if you're in a game where a 6 or 8 is rolled, and you can lay even-money against it being made, bet what you can against either of these numbers. You'll have a 9.09 percent edge.

That's my advice in nutshell. Bet wrong, then give odds against the 6 and 8 at even-money. You've got to be a winner unless you hit an extraordinary unlucky streak or unless the dice are crooked. Which brings me to my next bit of advice. Be very careful when playing in private dice games. The game could be fixed and the dice could be tampered with. If they bounce in strange ways, or you think they do, or if you have any doubts whatsoever about the honesty of the game or the players, get out of the game. A winner doesn't need action at all costs. The loser's philosophy is "Yes, I know its crooked, but its the only game in town." It's a funny remark, but losing is never fun.

XIII. SYSTEMS

A system is a methodical betting plan used in an attempt to overcome the house advantage in a particular gambling game or activity. Usually, a system is a progressive series of bets, done by increasing bets after losses, so that the ultimate winning bet will either wipe out previous losses, cut previous losses, or show a profit.

Systems are useless in games in which a player has an advantage over the house, such as blackjack, or in games in which a skillful player has an advantage over other opponents, such as gin rummy or poker. Therefore, when we discuss systems, we will discuss their application only to those games in which the player is at a disadvantage, such as craps, baccarat, or horse racing.

To even discuss a system for a game in which skill is the determining factor is a waste of time. When skill is the main determinant in play, then skill should be used as the foremost tool, without any reliance on betting systems.

An intelligent method of betting, such as outlined in the section on craps, by making use of the best possible odds, is not a system, and an increase in bets based on a correct counting of cards in blackjack is likewise not a system. Don't confuse methods and systems. *Methods of play and betting pay off in wins. Systems are the great destroyers of gamblers;* they delude gamblers into thinking that they can win just on luck, and no one wins on luck alone. No one is that lucky, for luck evens out in the long run; and when Lady Luck shines for a while, this only means that eventually she will turn her face away for long periods of time.

Despite the many systems invented over the years to overcome the house or operator's advantage, none has yet been devised that actually works, that is a true winning system. All have serious flaws and will eventually fail. Let's examine some of the more popular systems and see the fallacy behind them.

Casino Games Systems

First, the most widely used system is known as the Martingale System. This is the simple one of doubling bets after every loss till there is a win. The winning bet cancels all the losing bets and leaves the gambler ahead the amount of his or her original bet. For example, if you bet $1 and lose, you double your next bet to $2; and if you lose that bet, you keep doubling. Suppose you lose six times in a row and win once, here's what will happen:

Bet	Cumulative Loss
$1	$1
2	3
4	7
8	15
16	31
32	63
64	Win

At this point, you've won $1. In looking at the cumulative loss, note that it's always $1 less than the next bet. Thus, if you go on after losing nine bets in a row, your tenth loss of $512 will indicate to you that you're behind $1,023, for your next bet will be $1,024. And if you win that bet, how much are you ahead? $1!

These numbers should convince anyone of the absurdity of this system. First of all, at most casinos, there is a betting limit of $500, so that the tenth bet couldn't be $512. It would have to be $500, and if the bet is won, you're still behind $12, so what's the point of all this heartache? There is no point, really.

At this time, some readers might ask, "But how many times can you lose 10 times in a row?" Not frequently, I agree, but when you do lose, you'll lose $1,023, and the law of large numbers states that before you win $1,023 in separate transactions using this system, the odds are greatly in favor of losing 10 bets in a row. If you have the time, try an even-money bet, and flip a coin betting an imaginary dollar on heads or tails. Double the bet when you lose, and see if you can accumulate $1,023 before you lose ten in a row by incorrect guesses. This will open your eyes, I'm sure. And remember, heads or tails is an even-money proposition. When you're using betting systems, you may be bucking a disadvantage of anywhere from 1.2 percent all the way up to 20 percent, and the chances of not getting destroyed by one bad losing streak are practically nil.

Grand Martingale is an even more hazardous system for gamblers who don't want to win just $1 after that long series of losses but instead want to win $1 for every spin of the wheel or roll of the dice. Thus you start with $1, and if you lose, you bet $3; $1 for the loss, $1 to break even, and $1 as profit. Your bets would look like this:

Bet	Cumulative Loss
$1	$1
3	4
7	11
15	26
31	57
63	120
127	247
255	502
511	1,013

By the ninth bet, you're already over the $500 mark, and your bet would be limited to $500, which would make you a $2 loser. Even if you bet $511 and won, you would have won $9. Would you bet $511 to win $9? Why should you? This system is a sure way to total destruction.

The D'Alembert or Cancellation System is another popular system designed to be used at roulette. Under this system, the idea is not to have one bet wipe out all the previous losing bets and make you a slight winner. Instead, the bets are gradually increased in amount so that, after ten losing bets, you are not behind $1,023. You have lost much less, but, of course, you cannot wipe out the losses with one win. The most common use of the D'Alembert System is as follows:

You start by writing down these numbers—1 2 3. You bet the total of the end numbers, or 1+3=4. If you win, you cross off the two end numbers, the total of which you have just bet. Now your sheet looks like this: ~~1~~ 2 ~~3~~. The number 2 is left. You bet 2 units, and if you win, you cross that off also, so now your sheet looks like this—~~1~~ ~~2~~ ~~3~~. Now you've won 6 units or dollars. Simple. What if you lose a bet?

You start again with 1 2 3, and bet 4 units, your total of the end numbers. If you lose, instead of crossing out anything, you add the losing bet, so your sheet now looks like this—1 2 3 4. Now you bet the two end numbers, 1+4, which totals 5. If you win, you cross them out, and your sheet looks like this—

1 2 3 4. Now you bet the remaining numbers, adding up to 5. If you lose, you put the 5 at the end. It looks like this now—2 3 5. You bet the totals of the end numbers, which is 7. If you win, you cross out 2 and 5, thus—2 3 5. Now you bet the 3, and if you win you cross out the 3, so your total sheet looks like this—1 2 3 4 5.

At this point you are again ahead 6 units or dollars, which is the total of all three beginning numbers. The idea behind this system is twofold. First, when losing, you increase your bets gradually, so that you're not doubling up losses. Secondly, everytime you win you cross off *two numbers,* and everytime you lose you add only *one number.* That's the point. You only have to win a little over one-third of the time to come out ahead. A marvelous system, the adherents say. Of course, the adherents who say this haven't played it for money or they'd be consulting their bankruptcy lawyers or wailing in their beers.

The trouble with this system is that when it goes bad, as all systems involving progressions do, the numbers can become astronomical. I'll now show a D'Alembert progression that actually occurred at a roulette table in Las Vegas. 1 2 3 4 5 6 8 10 11 14 15 17 23 25 33 36 42 58 75 83 105 125 167 183 241 299 324 366 491, at which point the two end numbers surpassed $500 (491+125=616) and the system player gave up. At that time he was behind $1,046, and in a condition approaching shock.

Several times during the course of play he came close to closing the system and winning the $6, but he never quite managed it. A $6 system is so ferocious and scary that it will wipe anyone out who uses it. Even a system utilizing the D'Alembert process starting at 1 1, with the first bet being merely $2, can quickly escalate to bankruptcy.

There is an interesting sidelight to the D'Alembert System. A roulette player named Norman Leigh, having decided correctly that all systems fail and that only gamblers, not casinos, go broke from playing systems, decided to utilize the D'Alembert System, one of the riskiest, by playing it as an anti-system. In his book *Thirteen Against the Bank,* he describes his method, which is simply to do the opposite of the system. Everytime he lost, he crossed off two numbers and everytime he won he added a number, so that he could never lose more than $6 in any closing of the system, but his wins could be infinite, up until he was stopped by the house limit.

To accomplish this, he put together a gambling team, and had the members play at different roulette tables and at different positions. One would play the high-low, the second the red-black, and the third the even-odd even-money bets. When any one of his team hit a winning streak, that streak paid off tremendously, making up for all the small losses by the other members. The team played in English and European casinos, utilizing the single zero and *en prison* rule, which gave the house an edge of 1.35 percent, much lower than the American wheel, which gives the house an advantage of 5.26 percent. The team made a fortune till they were barred from playing at all the casinos. It's an interesting study of the ineffectuality of systems turned to advantage.

Casinos love systems and look with delight at the players who work them out. That's because all systems are basically flawed or senseless, and all eventually lead to disaster. For example, some systems begin only after five passes in a row have been made at the dice table or where red has shown five times in a row at roulette. These systems are even more foolish because the dice and the wheel have no memory, and what has happened before has no bearing on what will happen next. The law of large numbers determines odds, and the law deals in the millions of spins, not in five or a dozen. When the gambler feels that black is due after five spins of red, black may already be ahead of red in the first million spins by 82,000 spins.

Another factor that stops gamblers cold when they try a system is the principle of gambler's ruin, which is, to state it briefly, "that for every attempt to increase capital by some specified factor and using some specified betting method (a progressive betting system) a gambler has a specified probability of success and a corresponding probability of ruin. And the greater the attempted increase factor, the greater the probability of ruin."

We saw this principle in action during the big loss mentioned playing the D'Alembert System, where slowly but surely the increased bets led to the ruin of the gambler, by depleting his capital for that system.

A great many people who read this book are sitting down right now trying to work out a sure-fire system for beating the ponies, the dice, the wheel, or whatever. They are sure losers, because there is no easy way to beat disadvantageous gambling games, and the delusion that one system will work is a fallacy untold thousands of people have gone broke trying to prove. Casino gambling systems don't work; avoid them at all costs.

Racetrack Systems

Systems abound at the racetrack and are based on either post position, betting favorites, or handicap methods of one sort or another, and sometimes on combinations of the above. What these systems generally have in common is a progressive method of betting, so that, after a loss, the next bet is increased to cover the previous loss and to make money from the current race being bet.

Many desperate gamblers use a variety of systems at the racetrack because they find that it is almost impossible to win by any one system. They try to handicap horses but realize that there are so many unknown factors that it is very difficult to figure out the winner by any plausible method. After discarding any attempt at handicapping, they may go with the "smart money," betting on horses the public likes or on horses that have had a last-minute infusion of money bet on them. One way or another, all methods of trying to beat the horses and all systems of betting at the racetrack are doomed to be failures. The reason is quite simple. Most tracks, depending on jurisdiction and tax revenue laws, take about 18 to 20 percent of the handle for each race as taxes, expenses, etc.

This disadvantage is just too much to overcome, and there are countless thousands who have gone broke trying to beat the races. Others have made fortunes selling handicap systems and methods to the hapless horse race bettors, who grasp at any straw, looking for the "one way" to beat the horses, other than with the proverbial whip. They never find that magic method, but their search continues till today, and many "sure-fire" systems are still heavily advertised and sold.

Systems at the racetrack are very dangerous because, unlike the gambling table, there is no limit on how large a bet a horseplayer may make. All tracks are geared to pari-mutuel betting, which means that the more money placed on a horse, the lower his odds go at payoff time; and so the track will book any bet made by a gambler.

There are systems based on post positions at the trotters, where post position is very important, and on handicapping methods or odds at the thoroughbred races, or sometimes on a combination of factors. No matter how the systems player twists and turns in his effort to win at the track, the track edge stares him in the face with its imponderable reality of a close to 20 percent disadvantage to the bettor. It's just too much to overcome.

Let's follow a simple progressive systems method to show the great dangers inherent in one. This system is based on betting the favorites in every race. We're going to take the average nine-race card prevalent at most tracks and show a day where the betting favorite doesn't win a race. This happens infrequently, but it does happen, and systems players, gearing their progressive bets to favorites, must realize that it will happen to them several times in the course of a meet, sometimes for two days running.

Favorites, ranging from 1–10 to 7–2, win about 35 percent of the time at all tracks, a little more than one out of every three races on the average; and with this low figure, there may be long stretches of time when they don't win at all. Let's then examine one day's betting when they all fail. The gambler in this case wants to make a steady living of $90 a day and thus wants to win $10 per race. In order to do this, he must bet sufficient amounts to win $10 for the first race, and if he loses that race must bet enough to overcome his losses and win $10 for each of the first two races, and so on.

Race	Favorite's Odds	Loss	Amount to Win	Bet
1.	5–2		$10	$4
2.	2–1	$4	24	12
3.	8–5	16	46	30
4.	9–5	46	86	50
5.	1–1	96	146	150
6.	2–1	246	306	150
7.	8–5	396	466	300
8.	6–5	696	776	650
9.	2–1	1,346	1,436	700
	Total loss	2,846		

If those figures aren't sobering enough, I don't know what is. From a $4 bet to a $700 bet. From a $4 loss to a $2,046 loss. One bad day and this systems player is wiped out, if he has a moderate bankroll. And think of the aggravation and the tension he had to undergo for the last five races, as his bets escalated.

Betting second choices, which come in 18 percent of the time, or betting inside post positions at the trotters where losing streaks are longer, is suicidal. There are some insane gamblers who put huge amounts on odds-on favorites for show only and after winning a few $2.10 or $2.20 payoffs lose thousands of dollars on one lost race. Any of these systems is terrible, and once a gambler embarks on progressive betting systems of whatever kind at the track, he or she is inviting bankruptcy, heart attacks, and worse.

WINNING

XIV. WINNERS AND LOSERS

In everyday life there are many definitions of winners and just as many, or perhaps more, of losers. There have been times when someone was pointed out to me as a winner and I'd stare dumbfounded. Was he really a winner? I'd ask, "Why do you say he's a winner?" And the person with me would answer, "He really scores with the ladies." I'd look over the "scorer" and see a flashy, arrogant man swaggering around and know in my heart, ladies or no, that man wasn't a winner by any definition of mine.

Or I remember in my youth working for a man who spoke of various people as "bad actors." I asked for a definition of "bad actor" and was told it meant a "loser, a nobody; someone who didn't have any money." I'd look at the man so described and he would seem to be a gentle and kindhearted person, who may not have been driven by ambition to coin dollars, but still, how could one be defined as a loser in such simple terms?

I could go on with example after example. We may see a

celebrity on television and say inwardly, "My God, this woman has the world in her hands. She's a winner. If only I were like her," and then be shocked to hear that she's attempted suicide ten days later. Many of the celebrities the world admired, such as Marilyn Monroe and Freddie Prinze, to name just two, have had their personal torments and couldn't really deal with their own lives. To anyone on the outside, they were winners in every sense of the word, for they had looks, fame, recognition, talent, riches, and were adulated and sought after. But who knows what was secretly in their hearts? Who really knows what opinion they truly had of themselves?

Who are the real winners in life, and who are the losers? It's a discussion that could fill ten volumes and encompass all the philosophies and religions of the world, and in the end all we'd get would be conflicting opinions. To gain riches is a sign of success, one might write, and another, that riches are a sign of a failed life of the spirit. Contentment with one's lot in life is success, one philosopher states, and still another writes that when you are content, you are all but dead.

Philosophical definitions aside, in gambling, defining a winner is a simple matter. All we have to do is look at the gambler's bankroll. If it has increased as a result of playing, that person is a winner or is winning. If it has decreased in value, that person is losing or is a loser. No matter what excuses are given, no matter how wonderful that person is, if the bottom line shows a loss, he or she is losing. We have to suspend our humanistic definitions when we deal with gambling, for gambling results are simply figured out coldly, on paper.

If a man has won a million dollars playing, and we consider him a miserable human being, we must still think of him as a winner as far as gambling is concerned. If he has lost a million dollars and is a great human being, he is a loser. We cannot allow ourselves to be sidetracked by the other definitions we have of winners and losers, not in gambling. We must always look at that final bottom line.

As will be seen, however, most winners at gambling have certain favorable traits that make them winners, and most losers have unfavorable traits which hurt them. Often, gamblers who avoid unfavorable traits are on their way to becoming winners, for if they don't have the bad traits, they will automatically have the good, winning traits. It's like defining a dishonest person. There are hundreds of nuances and traits the dishonest person has, open to endless discussions, but an honest person is simply defined—he or she is honest. Period.

We're not trying to be philosophers here, but realists, and we'll examine those traits that prevent a man or woman from becoming a winner. The chapter on losing traits is one of the longest in the book, for it is one of the most important in the book, and I'm sure some of you will find to your dismay that many of the traits apply to you. If so, you owe it to yourself to get rid of them.

Remember that no one is doomed to always be a loser, and no one has the magic to always be a winner, for life is dynamic, and people change. Therefore, if you see you have losing traits, you can and should change them; and if you aren't guilty of these bad habits, study them anyway, to ensure that you never fall into their grasp.

Losing Traits

COMPLAINING ABOUT BAD LUCK

The whiners and complainers are nearly always losers. Many times, they plan their complaints and excuses in advance, for they are sure they're going to lose. These people are not really interested in winning, anymore than hypochondriacs are interested in staying healthy, for, if they won, then most of their daily lives, which consist of complaints and excuses, would be empty.

When you hear people complaining and making excuses after a losing session, you can be sure they're losers most of the time, not only for that session. I'm not saying that one should be a good loser, but, after losing, it's best to evaluate what went wrong, rather than simply to look for external excuses and complain of bad luck. This may happen once or twice, but when it happens over and over again, you should realize that you have very little interest in winning. What you really want to do is lose and complain, and seek excuses for your "bad luck."

THE ATTITUDE OF "EASY COME, EASY GO"

As any astute gambler knows, it's more difficult to have a big win than a big loss. Several factors must come together for you to win, but losing can be for any number of individual reasons. When you lose heavily, you often are wiped out before you even have a chance to draw a deep breath, for one reason or another. In poker, you might have gotten good cards, but the others have had slightly better cards. In blackjack, you might have been in several good counting situations with the deck very favorable, and yet your heavy bets and double downs were useless against the dealer's monster cards. This can happen and when it does, you just can't do anything about it.

Usually, when I've had a really big win, it has taken a long time to accumulate the money, but I've sustained large losses in very short time spans. Therefore, I know that to say "easy come, easy go," is to say I'm not interested in being a winner. *It doesn't come easy, and it shouldn't go easy.* When you've won big money, hold on, and don't go crazy with it. When you have the casino's money, use that money wisely. If you take $1,000 to the table and win $5,000, why risk that $5,000 all at once, when it probably will enable you to set a base for bigger bets and future winnings? Invest that $5,000 wisely in gambling, and you may find yourself ahead permanently from that time on.

TAKING CHANCES WITH MONEY AT HAND

When you reach into your pocket or wallet and say to yourself, "I've got $100; I'm going to take a chance with it," you are well on your way to losing. What you're really saying is "I'm going to get a few moments of thrills by creating some anxiety for myself, and I'll lose this $100 in the process." That's not the way to win.

Never sit in on any game with "scared" or inadequate money. You're better off walking past the game rather than risking a sum of money that one small streak of bad luck will wipe out. You're much better off preserving that money for the next time you're going to play seriously, with adequate funds. I've seen the same scene so many times, I could patent it. A man is walking through a casino. He goes by a table and takes out a hundred dollar bill, gets some chips in large denominations, and bets half his chips on the cards or dice. He loses, bets the other half, and loses that and gets up and walks on. Blown a hundred dollars in less than a minute. He probably feels lousy and more than that, stupid. And he is stupid to bet that way.

GAMBLING WITHOUT A BASIC PLAYING AND MONETARY STRATEGY

Before playing, carefully prepare for the game and know what your overall strategy will be. If you don't, you can wind up a heavy loser. In discussing this, another scenario comes to mind. I had a friend in Vegas who was a craps dealer at one of the downtown clubs. He had invited me to lunch and I was a little early and was standing near his craps table, watching the action. The game was a small one, with mostly $1 chips on the layout, but any craps game can become a big one with a high roller involved. A nondescript man wearing a plaid shirt walked by. He reached into his pocket and took out a hundred dollar bill.

He put the bill on the Field Bet. The next throw was a 7 and so he lost that bet. Now he bet $200 on the Field Bet, pulling out a big roll of bills from his pocket. Another 7 was rolled. Another loser. Behind $300, he peeled off some more cash and bet $300 on the pass-line, saying aloud, "No sense in fighting the dice." The next roll was a 4, but he didn't take odds, for he was just trying to get out even, and a 7 came right back. So now he was down $600. To make a long story short, he dropped $20,000 while I waited for my friend to get his lunch break.

He dropped it not only because of bad luck but because of bad bets. He bet the Field and proposition bets and in desperation to get even, he covered all the outside place numbers on the layout, hoping for a miracle. His betting had no rhyme or reason and was completely disorganized. Never do what he did. You must not only know what you're going to bet but the way you'll be utilizing your money on the best bets; otherwise your chances of winning will be nil, and your game will deteriorate into chaos.

INCREASING BETS WHILE LOSING

If you're playing at a certain betting level, never increase that betting level if you're losing. If possible, lower it, or better yet, leave the table after you've reached a certain losing position in terms of your bankroll. If you don't do this, you're going to be in big trouble. Suppose you've been making $5 bets at the blackjack table and the cards have been going against you. The deck has remained unfavorable and it seems as if every upcard the dealer holds is a 10 or ace.

However, you know something about correct play, and you've limited your losses to $90 at this point. You look at your watch. It's 2:50 PM and you have an appointment at 3:30. Well, you say to yourself, I'll get even in a hurry and get out of here.

You feel a little bad about losing $90, but the cards can't keep up this way, can they? No one answers your secret question; so you pull out some cash, a couple of $100 bills and now buy $25 chips. You bet $50 and get fresh cards off the top of the deck. Two wins, you tell yourself, and you'll be even and a few bucks ahead. But you don't win the first $50 bet or the second one either. Finally, as the cards continue to stay bad, you miss the 3:30 appointment, which now seems trivial, in view of the fact that you're down close to $1,200. And still the cards haven't improved.

I point out this and other horror stories not because I want to frighten anyone but because they happen all the time. That's why the casinos grow more opulent all the time. That's why new ones are built and old ones are constantly being remodeled and enlarged. They're doing it on your money, *on your money*. That's not fair. You should be taking their money for once; but, playing like my not-so-imaginary character in this example, you can't help but be a loser.

A year ago, I was watching a friend play blackjack at the Landmark Hotel in Las Vegas. She was at a $2 table and I was pointing out the fine points of the game since she was a beginner. We were the only ones at the table and so I sat next to her and leisurely told her what to do.

She was winning a few dollars when a man in his early fifties, wearing a cheap pair of workpants and a torn shirt, suddenly sat down to play. He bet $2 a hand for a few hands, losing them. Without warning, he emptied his wallet and bet $500 on the next hand. The game was being played with four decks, dealt out of a shoe, and the dealer turned and looked for the floorman. "Cash on the table," he said, aloud. The floorman looked at the big bet. I looked at the bet and the man making it. Was there something he knew that I didn't know? I had been counting cards on behalf of my friend and at that moment the deck was very unfavorable to the players.

"Deal the cards," the floorman said to the dealer, while he

stood and watched the action. A few people drifted by and were now grouped behind the man, attracted by all that cash on the table.

"Money plays," said the dealer. He slid the cards out of the shoe. The player received two 6s (since the cards were dealt open, I could follow the play), and the dealer showed an 8 as his upcard. The player split the 6s and placed another $500 on the table. It was a bad play and now I knew the player had just gone off the wall with his bet.

He got a 9 on the first 6, which would have given him a 21 if he hadn't split. He looked at his 15 for a long time and then stood pat. He got a 10 on the other 6 and stood with 16, both bad plays. The dealer had a 2 underneath his 8 for a 10; hit and dealt a 4 for 14. I watched the player's face. It was tight and his eyes were narrowed with regret, as he knew that 4 would have given him 20 on his second bet. Then the dealer slid out another card, turned over a 3, and stood on his 17. The player, having lost both his bets, stood up, nearly falling off his feet, and staggered away.

I can't repeat this advice strongly enough. Don't change betting limits, not when you're losing. And don't go crazy with your bets on wild hunches. *Hunches are what the loser depends on. The winner depends on skill.*

SHOWING OFF WITH BIG BETS

Don't confuse your personal worth with your gambling prowess, and don't show off to assert that worth. There are many people who think that making big bets, bets beyond their means, is some kind of status symbol. These are the same inadequate people who go into hock to rent luxurious houses. They're not impressing anyone but their creditors.

Back to gambling. I was playing blackjack at the Horseshoe in downtown Las Vegas where I've always done quite well. It was a $5 minimum table, early on a Monday morning, and the table was unoccupied—just myself against the dealer, head to head. I like to play 21 alone, since I know there's only one good player at the table, and no one to make stupid plays, such as splitting 10s and taking away good cards from the deck in favorable situations.

I was betting in the $25 to $100 range and was ahead quite a bit when this young man sat down at the table. He was in his early twenties, slim, good looking, with tousled dark hair. He had come with a young woman and another male friend, and his companions asked the dealer if they could sit down and watch their friend play, without playing themselves. The dealer agreed, for the casino at 3 AM was pretty deserted.

The player cashed in $200 and made a $5 bet as the cards were being reshuffled. When he saw my $50 bet, he asked me how I was doing. I shrugged, for I never want to brag about winning, not with a dealer present. The young man told his companions he was going to break the casino and raised his bet to $25, then he looked over at me, as though his increased bet either impressed me or made us buddies.

A cocktail waitress came over, and they all ordered drinks. I hardly ever drink when I gamble, and I didn't see why I had to drink because he was drinking, though he felt he had to make a $25 bet because I was betting with the green $25 chips.

The game went on. The young man was an average player, which is to say he was going to lose moderately. He didn't know the fine points of the game, and he wasn't counting cards. The cards remained favorable, and after about forty five minutes of play I was winning another $800. A floorman drifted over and watched the game.

The young man was winning also, but he was getting drunk, and showing off to his companions by doubling his bet after each win. He ran into a bad streak and started losing, and he began doubling his bets after each loss. He dropped the original $200 and took out another $200, and that went also. More drinks came. Emboldened by liquor, he decided to show his friends that he wasn't a penny-ante player. After losing this $200, he asked the woman for money. She protested; then when he told her with bravado that it was "only money" and that she was acting like a scared woman, he made three big bets on the layout and miraculously won all three. He left the doubled money on the table. The dealer told him it was over the $500 betting limit, but the floorman told the dealer it was OK, to deal the cards.

He was bombed out on the next hand as the dealer turned over a blackjack. Now the young man borrowed money from his male friend and lost that; then he reached into his wallet and found a $50 bill after much searching and lost that. He got up from the table, spilling his drink in the process, as he tried to swagger off, but who was he kidding? I knew he was a stupid fool and the dealer knew it, and the floorman, now using a napkin to wipe off the table, knew it.

Remember, you don't have to impress anyone at the table. The dealers have all seen bigger bettors than you, and the floormen have seen bigger losers; so play within your own limits. And you're not impressing anyone by being a big loser. When you run out of money by being an idiot, you'll end up being despised or pitied, not admired for having bet heavily. Don't show off. Don't brag. Be unobtrusive. The gambling table isn't the place to play status games.

DRINKING OR TAKING DRUGS WHILE GAMBLING

The movie image of the hard drinking poker player gathering in all the chips is not a realistic one. I watched the finals of the World Championship of Poker a couple of years ago, and not one of the finalists had anything stronger than a cup of coffee in front of him. The best poker players don't drink when playing. Just a little alcohol, they realize, takes the edge off their perceptions and this edge is what they bring to the game.

On the other hand, in all the years I've been watching people gamble, I've seen plenty of big drinkers at poker tables and 90 percent of the time they were losers. There is no way that drinking can help you at the table. Occasionally, if you want to have one weak drink to loosen you up, that's fine, but anything more and you're asking for trouble. Two immediate things happen when you drink. One, your senses are dulled, and two, you lose your inhibitions. Both are deadly sins at a gambling table.

When your senses are dulled, you lose the ability to think clearly and correctly. It may not hurt you that much in a mechanical game like baccarat or craps, where you make the same kind of bets over and over again; but in any thinking game, especially poker, you're at the mercy of the other players. When good players see a drunk at a poker table, they turn into a swarm of sharks, cutting and biting and ripping and grabbing what they can. A whole table can feast off one drunk, wiping him out. Who wants to be that kind of victim?

The other bad thing is loss of inhibition. Drinking makes the weak brave, but it's a false bravery. It is caution thrown to the winds. And you can't do that in fast moving gambling games where a lot of money can be lost in a hurry. When you lose your inhibitions, you start to make wild, crazy bets, and then, without even knowing what you are doing, you may, if you have credit at a casino, use it all up in one wild binge and, waking up the next day with a splitting headache, realize that you must have done something foolish, because you're broke and feeling *so bad*.

To top it off, alcohol is also a depressant. It may rev you up for a little while, but inevitably it has the opposite effect, a real down effect. If you're playing long enough, first you'll lose control of your senses, then your inhibitions, then you'll get depressed. Playing while depressed is like playing with a gun at your head; there's no hope for clear thinking with that much anxiety hanging over you. As will be shown more clearly in another chapter, any decisions made under depression tend to be destructive.

Drinking is bad enough, but when you use drugs and gamble, you're asking for big big trouble. Your senses and perceptions become completely disorganized, and what seems like normal activities under the influence of drugs, might be, in reality, activities and moves that are leading you to ruin. *You can't play normal games in abnormal states.* I'm not a preacher and I don't really care what you do in privacy, but this book is written to make you a winner at gambling, and you can't do it on coke, on uppers or downers, on pot, on bennies, on speed, or even on heavy medication.

If you have to take drugs, even simple things like antihistamines, don't gamble. They'll make you drowsy and you won't function properly. Any drug will change you, and when you're not your normal self, avoid the one activity that can really hurt you—and that's gambling.

PLAYING WITHOUT COMPREHENSION

Don't play in a game that you don't truly understand, or one where the rules are strange to you, or where they are too complicated for your immediate comprehension.

This may sound like elementary stuff, but I've seen untold craps players who didn't even know they could take single or double odds on their line bets and didn't know how to make a come bet, yet there they were, emptying their wallets of cash to get some action going.

In blackjack, the situation is worse, because blackjack is a game that can be beaten. At the worst, you play even with the house, and with correct basic strategy and counting cards, you have a decided advantage over the casino. Yet, blackjack continues to function in the casinos as a lucrative game for the house. Why is that? How can that be when the game can be beaten? That's because most people playing don't even know the correct basic strategy. And of those who do, many of them haven't learned the self-control and money management we stress in this book and mismanage their money so that they lose with wild and incredible bets.

And many others, in whatever game they play, don't really want to win. They want action and get bored with steady wins. They go off winning methods and go crazy with outlandish bets.

So be careful. Don't play any casino game that you don't know thoroughly and that you don't have a sound basic strategy for. As to a game like poker, always be more skilled than the opposition; otherwise there's no hope of winning over the long run. This is a hard world, as you must know by now, and the gambling world is harder than any other world. There's no mercy. If you aren't better than your opponents, they'll quickly dispose of you.

It's not enough in poker to know the elementary rules and some strategy. You must know more. Study the poker sections in this book as starters. To win, you have to know as much about the game as you can, and you have to play at a betting level where your knowledge is superior to the other players. It's as simple as that, and yet, that simple basic premise isn't followed by the vast majority of poker players. *That's why there are so many more losers than winners.* And, as Barnum said, "There's a sucker born every minute." But not many know the end of that sage statement ". . . and two to take him." Don't be taken. Know what you're doing.

DISCARDING WINNING METHODS THROUGH IMPATIENCE AND GREED

If you find that you have a winning method, stay with it. Be patient. Don't change it through impatience. There is a tendency for most gamblers to become greedy while gambling. Having worked out a sure-fire method for continual wins, they deviate because of greed and impatience and find themselves losing not only all their hard-gained wins but their bankroll as well.

I had a private gambling pupil who did quite well at blackjack in Las Vegas. One of the chief concerns when playing blackjack is to be barred from the game as a card counter, and thus I worked out with Jim, as I'll call him, a slow and gradual method of raising his bets when the deck was favorable to the players.

Jim played with $5 casino chips and thus didn't draw any heat from casino personnel. Under my method, he was winning about $100 a day on average, day in and day out. He played no more than three or four hours a day, and in a few weeks had accumulated over $2,000 in winnings. I eventually moved away from Las Vegas, while Jim kept playing there. Through some friends, I ran into Jim again in San Francisco and asked him how he was doing at the game. He shrugged his shoulders, which is always a negative sign.

"What does that mean?" I asked.

"Not so good."

"How much are you ahead?"

"Ahead?" He gave a wry laugh.

"What happened?"

Then the story came out. Not satisfied with the method I had worked out for him, Jim got greedy and in every favorable situation, no matter how slight, he increased his bets tenfold. This drew immediate attention from pit bosses and he was barred from several casinos. Not only was this foolish, but Jim was betting way out of proportion to the favorable situations. As a result of his attempts to make a lot of money as fast as possible, he lost some big bets, and then, finding his winnings evaporating, he increased his basic bets to $50 without a sufficient bankroll. Then, finding himself in a temporary losing streak, he made a few outlandish bets, lost his bankroll, and was wiped out.

I couldn't believe it, yet I could believe it. I had gone over money management with him carefully, but Jim was too impatient to listen. All he had to do was stay patient and he could have made at least $30,000 and possibly as much as $50,000 that year. But he became bored with winning steadily, and he lost everything because *he couldn't stand to win;* he became impatient and greedy.

Jim could have increased his bets only when his bankroll called for it. I had him divide the initial bankroll into ten parts. He had started with about $2,000. When his bankroll hit $5,000 he could have increased his normal bet from $5 to $10, and slowly increased it as he continued to win and add to it.

I had explained all this to him beforehand, but his impatience and greed won out in the end, to his sorrow. *Impatience and greed: the key words of a loser, not only at the tables, but in life.* Remember these two words and don't be victims of them. Patience is a wonderful virtue, and its wonders are nowhere seen to better effect than at the gambling table.

XV. MONEY MANAGEMENT

Money management, in terms of gambling, is not a simple expedient of betting and either winning or losing, then taking a final tally. If you handle gambling money in such an offhand manner, you're not going to be a winner. The most important thing to remember is that managing the money you gamble with correctly is as vital as knowing the best strategies of the game you're playing.

If you're playing poker and have studied the game carefully, so that you're a skilled and knowledgeable player, but you have one losing session that wipes out your entire bankroll, then all your knowledge and skill is worthless, because you can't play poker without money. Handling and controlling money, managing your gambling stake or bankroll, is to be studied and taken as seriously as studying the correct moves in any gambling game.

Money management is divided into several parts, as follows:

- The total amount of money used for gambling purposes—your bankroll.
    a. The long-term bankroll.
    b. The short-term bankroll.
- The percentage of the total bankroll used for a single session of gambling.
- The betting limits to be followed.
- How much you can afford to lose in a single session.
- How much you should win at a single session.
    a. How to segregate your winnings at the table.
- When to raise your betting stakes when winning.

Casino Games

THE TOTAL BANKROLL

The bankroll used for gambling will vary from person to person, depending on his or her financial resources, and there is no set percentage that I can arbitrarily name.

However, *money used for gambling purposes should never be money that you cannot afford to lose.* Now when I write about a sum that you can afford to lose, I don't expect that you'll lose it. You're gambling to win, not to lose, but there is no guarantee that you will win, no matter how skillfully and carefully you play; for, in a short period of time, luck can swing violently against you. In the long run, using the principles outlined in this book, you're going to be a winner, but in the course of a short period of play, anything can happen.

Before deciding to gamble, put aside a bankroll that will be sufficient for the betting limits you are comfortable with. The bankroll will also be determined by the length of time you are willing or able to gamble. If you decide to gamble professionally for a living, obviously you'll need a larger bankroll than if you're going to be at a resort like Las Vegas for a weekend.

• *Long-term gambling.* By this term I don't mean a lifetime of gambling, but perhaps a season of football betting or a few months at a casino playing blackjack. In these situations, if you can't afford to put away sufficient money to make the gambling worthwhile, don't gamble at all.

Wait for your bankroll to catch up to your desire to play the games for the stakes you'll be comfortable with. Don't rush things. Suppose you decide to bet the coming football season seriously, with the hopes of making several thousands in winnings. If you have a limited bankroll of a thousand dollars, you're not going to be able to do this. You should either wait for a larger bankroll or lower your expectations by making smaller bets.

For example, with $1,000 as your bankroll, you decide to make a number of $100 bets on football games, betting even more when there is a "sure thing." With a limited $1,000 bankroll, a few losses and you'll be out of business.

In betting on sports events, you should have enough for at least forty losing bets in a row before being tapped out. We know the odds are horrendous against losing forty bets in a row, but if you lose two out of three bets continually, plus pay the vigorish, before you know it, your bankroll will be nil. If you do go broke betting football in spite of having forty times your normal bet in reserve, then you're inadequately prepared in terms of strategy. Don't blame your losses on luck or money or whatever. Blame it on the fact that you don't know enough about football to beat the bookies.

As to long-term betting, here are the minimum amounts you should have ready before you play or bet any games on a serious basis. All reserve figures that follow are the bare minimum.

a. Sports betting. Have at least 40 times your usual bet in reserve. If your normal bet is $100, have $4,000 behind that bet.

b. Casino games. In craps, have at least 500 times your

ordinary line bet in reserve. If you're betting $10, have at least $5,000 in reserve.

In blackjack, have at least 500 times your neutral or opening bet in reserve. If your neutral bet is $10, then you should have at least $5,000 in reserve.

c. Poker. For long-term play, you should have at least 500 times the maximum bet at the game. If you're in a maximum $20 game, then you must have $10,000 in reserve.

All of these figures may seem high to you, yet I'm tempted to raise them even higher. What I've stated are *minimum reserve figures,* not the maximum.

The more you have behind you in reserve, the more likely you'll weather losing streaks of long duration, and the more likely you'll remain levelheaded and cool in the face of adversity.

You must have enough of a reserve not only to withstand the losing streaks but also to always have enough money available so that you won't be tempted to alter your betting strategy when you're on a losing streak.

• Short-term play. Most of us are not professional gamblers but people who like to play on occasion. Perhaps you're going away for a weekend to the Caribbean, Atlantic City, or Vegas. Perhaps you want to make some bets during the basketball season or you have a weekly poker game. Even though you're not interested in making a living out of gambling, you should still give serious consideration to your bankroll. Again, you must think of a total stake for your limited play, based on the limits you're comfortable with.

For example, suppose that you arrange to stay five days and four nights in Las Vegas. The game you intend to play is blackjack, and you decide to set aside $600 for gambling purposes on this trip. If your usual bet is $10, and you bring only $600 with you, you'll find yourself undercapitalized and will be playing with scared money. After one losing session, your $600 bankroll can either disappear or be severely dented, and you'll find the rest of your stay boring and nerve-wracking. There are other things to do in Las Vegas besides gamble, but with the constant action at the tables you'll go out of your mind. You came here to play the tables, not to spend all your time at the pool or eating.

Even if you've salvaged $100 of that initial bankroll, you'll be afraid to raise your bets in advantageous situations because there's just not enough money on hand, and altering your betting strategy in 21 so that you can't take advantage of favorable situations can be devastating.

Bring only money you can afford to lose for the short stay, but at least bring a sufficient amount for your style of play. If you're betting $10 as a neutral bet, you should have at least 400 times that bet, or $4,000 for gambling.

What if you can spare only $600 for gambling purposes? Fine, but don't make $10 neutral bets. All you'll be able to bet, using our formula, is $1 to $2 as your neutral bet. At this point you might ask, who wants to bet pennies? What's the whole point of playing then? I understand your feelings very well, but realistically, that's all you can afford to bet. If you bet at higher limits, one bad streak and you'll be wiped out. It's best to win $50 by overcoming temporary streaks and sticking to a winning strategy than it is to blow $600 in one day through one bout of bad luck and spend the rest of the vacation climbing the walls.

For all short-term play, no matter what the game, you should have at least four-fifths of the long-term bankroll available. We're again talking about the minimum long-term bankroll. If your bet at craps on the line is $10, then you'll need $4,000 as your reserve. It's a simple formula, but again, only a formula. Its purpose is to prevent you from playing with scared money, so that your whole style of play will alter to accommodate your limited funds. You can't play correctly or boldly without sufficient reserves, and if you try to play this way, your chances of winning are negligible. It's as simple as that.

THE PERCENTAGE OF TOTAL BANKROLL USED FOR EACH SESSION OF PLAY

If you bring $2,000 with you for a weekend of play at blackjack or craps, you now know that you cannot bet more than $5 as your neutral bet in blackjack, where your range of bets might be $2 to $10. In craps, you would be betting $5 as a line or come bet with equivalent odds. (If you're in a double odds game, then you should have $2,500, or 450 times your ordinary line bet.)

Before you start play, divide your bankroll into ten equal parts, and allot $200 for a session of blackjack, where your neutral bet is $5. The neutral bet or line bet is always one-fortieth of your single session bankroll. Once you bring this bankroll to the table, you never lose more than this amount at any one session of play, remembering the wise adage that the first loss is the cheapest loss.

The reason for splitting the total bankroll into ten equal parts this way is twofold. First, you're limiting your losses at any one table, keeping a strong reserve for future play. Suppose you do lose $200 in your first session. Well, you still have the bulk of your cash in reserve, $1,800 in your pocket. Suppose you lose three times in a row? You still have $1,400 in reserve, plenty of money to make a strong comeback and to come out a winner.

Your second reason for dividing the money into ten equal parts has to do with the unfavorability of play at a particular table. If you're playing blackjack, for instance, you might find the cards running against you, and you're automatically out of the game once you've lost your $200 or 10 percent of your total bankroll. The loss is telling you a story—you're at a bad table. Time to leave.

The formula for the initial bankroll and the subsequent division of that bankroll into ten parts for individual sessions are all safety measures that will protect and ultimately benefit you.

THE BETTING LIMITS TO BE FOLLOWED

In any game of chance you must utilize those betting limits that allow you the most leverage and also that will keep you in the game for the longest possible time so that you aren't tapped out by the time luck turns your way. On the other hand, you don't want to play at such a low betting limit or one so below your comfortable range of betting that the game becomes meaningless and boring. If you bring $2,000 with you for a weekend's play at craps, you don't want to get into $1 games.

Once you know your single session bankroll, you then divide that figure by 40 to find out your betting limits. If you have a single session bankroll of $200, you make $5 neutral bets in blackjack and $5 line bets in craps. Four hundred dollars permits $10 neutral bets in 21 and $10 line bets in craps, and so forth. When at a table, I give myself an even bigger leeway, adding another $100 to my single session play. I would bring $500 to a table when I make $10 netural bets in blackjack, and overall, my total bankroll is $1,000 higher than the $4,000 necessary. Many times that extra $100 turned the tide in my favor. I want a little more, rather than a little less, when I face the enormous resources of a casino.

HOW MUCH CAN YOU AFFORD TO LOSE IN A SINGLE SESSION?

We've already covered this in the previous discussions, but it's of such vital importance that we'll go over it once again. You should never lose more than what you bring to a single session of play, and the important rule is that *you must never reach into your pocket once the single session stake is lost. Never!*

Thus, if you brought $500 to the table and lost it, you must leave the table. You never take out fresh money in this situation for several good reasons. You know that you're at a table where nothing is going your way. If you're playing blackjack, the composition of the deck, the manner in which the cards are placed in that deck, even in innocent shuffling, is working against you. Also, you tend to lose confidence after a long losing streak, and you may be unconsciously altering your bets to preserve money. You might not double down on an 11 if the dealer is showing a 10, even though it's a good play in favor of the player. In craps, you might be afraid to take odds on your line and come bets on difficult points, such as 4 or 10. Instead of taking out fresh money or altering your play, you must assume that a particular game can't be beaten this session, and you must get out of the game.

When you've lost your single session stakes, leave the table with a clear head. Don't brood about it. Don't think about past losses. Look to the future. The losers are always complaining about the bad luck they've encountered in the past, and the winners are preparing for the future. Everyone will lose at one time or another. It can't be helped. Go away from the table with the idea of refreshing yourself. Have a meal or coffee or a mild drink. Go back to your room and rest or read a magazine or book. Or better yet, get some exercise. Take a long walk or go for a swim or play some tennis. Break the losing spell and come back later for another session of play with a clear head and a relaxed spirit.

Sometimes, though this will be rare, you might be playing at a card game where either the dealer or the players are cheating you by manipulation of the cards or by partnerships signaling each other, as often happens in big poker games. You may have no knowledge of the cheating going on, except that you lose pot after pot or hand after hand. You don't know the reason for your swift and drastic losses, but the loss itself waves a red flag in front of your eyes. *You must get out of any game where nothing is going right.*

When things are going badly, in any game, you don't have to wait until your very last dollar is lost in order to leave the table. For instance, at a craps table, you might find yourself down to $60 after a starting bankroll of $500. Suppose you've been making a line bet of $10, taking odds of $10, and making two $10 come bets, also taking single odds. Your $60 will last for the line and two come bets with odds, a full cycle, but you find to your dismay that the first bet on the line is lost as the shooter rolls a craps. Now you are left with $50, and in order to finish your cycle of one line bet and two come bets with odds, you'll have to take money out of your pocket. *At that moment, leave the table.* Limit your losses. And limit them without resorting to extra funds from your reserve.

Don't ever put yourself in a position where you'll be forced to take money from your pocket. Save the $50 for the next session of craps, and start fresh at a table where things couldn't possibly be worse and might be a lot better than this dismal table.

As a footnote to all this I'll mention a very common situation that practically all gamblers have encountered. After a long losing session where you are down to your last few bucks, the cards or dice turn your way, and you come back all the way until you're even once more and now have your original single session bankroll intact again. What should you do now?

After long experience and many interviews with gamblers of all types, I'm going to give you the best advice I can in this situation. If you've had a long losing streak and then you've come back to your original starting bankroll, that is, you're even again, *get out of the game.*

You've been worn out by the losing streak, and usually, its been a long haul to get even again. You're tired and beat. The worst thing to do is linger on and try to win. Just as rapidly as the cards or dice have come your way, they can turn into another losing cycle. By coming back even, you've nursed a tremendous winning streak, and winning streaks don't last forever. The message is clear. Get out of the game. Get away from the table.

It's a terrible feeling to come back all the way from a long loss and then find the money draining away once more. Don't let this happen to you. Once you're even, run for your life. Some authorities will tell you to remain in the game after you've gotten even again, otherwise you've wasted all that time without making any money. But if you've been almost broke all evening and now have your original bankroll, you've done well enough, and leave well enough alone.

HOW MUCH SHOULD YOU WIN AT A SINGLE SESSION?

Now let's look at the bright side of things. Suppose, instead of having a bad run, you start off winning and continue to win. How much should you leave the table with, and during that winning streak, what should you do with your winnings?

Always set an interim goal of doubling your money, but don't be satisfied with that goal alone. Having obeyed the maxim that you must limit your losses, you must also look at the other side of the coin and *let your winnings ride.*

There are different approaches to take in blackjack and craps, the casino games, because of the different betting structures of these two games. If you are in a dice game and betting with the dice, you will encounter, generally speaking, a number of small losses and usually one "hot roll," where points and numbers keep repeating and you take in a bundle of money. *Never count on more than one hot roll in a dice game in any one session.*

After that one hot roll is over, leave the table immediately, and don't look back. There are times that you'll be way ahead without a really hot roll, where the 7 will show infrequently and most of your points will repeat. Let's say you started with $500 and now have $920—not quite double your money but close enough, and of course, at this moment you don't really know what the future at the table will hold for you. The dice might get cold, but, on the other hand, the really hot roll is just around the corner.

If you had been betting with the dice and making $10 line and come bets and also taking odds, your method of playing a line and two come bets with odds calls for a $60 cycle. Having won $420, I'd now suggest that you put away all but $120 of your money, and use the $120 for future betting. This will leave you enough for two complete betting cycles. If you continue to win and accumulate more chips, keep the $120 segregated. When you lose two complete cycles of bets, and thus the $120, you must get out of the game.

However, keep in mind the next section of this chapter, dealing with the raising of stakes during a winning streak. But for all intents and purposes, when the $120 is gone, you must get away from the dice table. Never linger there to try your luck a little longer, for that would force you to reach into your pocket for the $500 you started with and the additional $300 in winnings you've put away.

To be a winner, and I'll repeat this statement often in this book, *you must quit a winner.* If you're winning during a session of play and you lose it back to the house without leaving the table, you're a loser, not a winner. The final count, the bottom line, is what is important. If you came to the table with $500 and left with $505, theoretically you're a winner; but if you were ahead $400 at one time, put away money, and then used it again, you're a loser in my book. The minute you tamper with money in your pocket, whether it's a reserve or winnings from the session, the money you're taking out I consider as lost money.

And if you came to the table with $500, ran it up to $2,000, got reckless, and lost all of your winnings and half of your original single sessions stake, even if you didn't pocket it, you're a loser. Once you're ahead, double your money or close to it, you've got to pocket money. Don't delude yourself. A winner is determined by his or her winnings, or, as a famous poker player is fond of saying, "You can always tell a hunter by his hides." That's the final, ultimate test. It's as simple as that.

Even if you're not doubling your money, you should think of leaving the table a winner. If after a long session of play starting with $500, you're ahead $150, start thinking of getting out. If you're tired at this point, leave out $60 for one more cycle and put away the $500 plus your winnings of $90. If the $60 or any part of it is lost, walk away. Ninety dollars isn't a fortune, but it certainly adds up, and gives you the casino's money to start the next session of play with.

Blackjack is a different type of game, and so you must use a different formula in preserving winnings. Here, there are no hot rolls to warm your heart. The game may evolve into a number of cycles, where you win for a while, then lose, then win again, and sometimes these cycles are of long duration. You never truly see the cycles until they're over, but this fact won't prevent you from protecting your winnings anyway.

Let's suppose that, as in the craps game, you've started with $500 and now have $920. At this point you should put away $800 and play out the $120. Whatever this $120 earns for you in additional profits goes into your pocket as well. Keep the $120 out and keep playing with it. When it is lost, you get out of the game a winner. However, keep in mind the next section of this chapter, on raising your stakes while winning.

There is nothing more disappointing or debilitating than to have won $500 or any large amount in blackjack by carefully keeping count of the cards and playing the correct blackjack strategies and then watching it all melt away, digging into your bankroll and watching that go as well.

When I see people who play this way, and the majority do it all the time, I know they're doomed to be losers. Anyone can leave a table with less than he or she came with after a losing streak, for this is natural to gambling; but the real losers, the ones who'll never be winners, leave with less even after winning a small fortune during the course of play.

Again, in blackjack as in any other game, you might not double your money or come close to doubling it. However, you should make provisions for leaving a winner. If I'm ahead $100 in a $10 neutral bet game, I decide in my mind to leave a winner, and I put away a $25 chip and play with the rest of the winnings. I want to leave with some of the casino's money, and this mind determination assures me I'll leave a winner. If the $75 evaporates, I walk away a winner. What a sweet feeling it is to always leave a winner. Get used to that feeling for it isn't hard to take at all.

WHEN TO RAISE YOUR BETTING STAKES WHEN WINNING

Anyone who's gambled has encountered those glorious sessions where everything went right, where no matter what was bet or what was played, luck was on his or her side. If you have that kind of session and don't take advantage of it, then you're as remiss as if you left the table broke after winning a fortune during the course of play.

In craps, when I'm in the middle of a hot roll I raise the come bets after they repeat. For example, if I'm making $10 line and come bets and taking single odds on the dice and I'm ahead $350 after starting with a bankroll of $500, I now make a usual $10 line bet and two $10 come bets and take single odds. If a come bet repeats, I raise it to $20 after my payoff and take $20 odds. I raise each come bet to $20 and if the line bet wins, I bet $20 on the line. During a hot roll, I keep raising the line and come bets by $10 increments, as long as the hot roll continues. At the end of some hot rolls, my original $10 bets have moved up to $100, with $100 odds.

Remember, a "hot roll" is not an abstract term. You know of its existence when numbers keep repeating and points are made. In other words, you know a hot roll when you're in the middle of one, for you're continually collecting and should be continually raising your bets.

Never anticipate a hot roll. That's what the losers do. They tell themselves, "This is it; I have the feeling the dice are going to get hot," and raise all their bets, and subsequently lose their shirts. That's the loser's psychology, anticipation. Winners only increase their bets when winning—with casino money.

There are people who say that the money you have in the rails at the craps table or the chips on the layout in the blackjack table is always your money, and to think of it as the casino's money is a fallacy. In one sense they're correct, but what they don't take into consideration is that you're there to gamble, and the money you have brought to the table is your stake.

If your stake is $500 at the outset of play and increases to $850, the additional $350 was the casino's, but it is now part of your gambling bankroll. To think of it as your own money rather than as part of your bankroll negates the whole idea of gambling. If you think that each $10 bet could be more wisely used for groceries, you would be better off not gambling. You must be confident and aggressive at the table and not think of the chips representing money or goods, your money and your goods, money you must hold onto at all costs. If that's the case, you shouldn't gamble.

So I repeat—bet aggressively with the money you've made from the casino. Anytime you're ahead an additional 50 percent of your original bankroll, start raising your bets; and at the same time, put away some winnings. If you started with $500 and now have $750, raise your neutral bet in blackjack to $15 from $10; and, at the same time, put away $100 of the winnings in your pocket.

Multiply the casino's money for your own purposes, for it's when you're winning that you should become aggressive and increase bets, not when you're losing. The winners know this and the losers don't; and often that's the only difference between the winners and the losers.

As you keep winning, increase your bets accordingly. Ride out the winning streak for all you can get. If you've turned that extra $150 in blackjack to $300, raise the neutral bet to $20 and keep raising it as you win. And keep putting away more and more of your winnings. When the streak is over, don't linger. Leave the table. This advice will hurt the casino's profit margins, not yours.

What one must be careful with in raising bets is not to do it prematurely, so that it jeopardizes winnings. Don't raise your bets if one bad streak will deplete all your winnings. There should always be a reserve that can be put away as permanent winnings from that session before your bets are increased.

Poker and Other Forms of Gambling

I have concentrated on the casino games because they're the easiest to control as far as money management goes, and they are the games most people will be playing for a period of time, usually on a continuous basis for a weekend or longer. However, in any gambling endeavor, don't play with money you can't afford to lose. And divide the money you are gambling with into ten equal parts if you want to play a weekend of poker at a casino or poker parlor or club. If you're winning at poker and the players are inferior to you, stay as long as you're winning. Stay for two days if you can keep awake and alert and keep winning.

However, in any gambling pursuit, you must not only conserve your capital, but you must make sure to quit a winner. I can't repeat this often enough. So if you're ahead $500 in a poker game and thus have doubled your money, put $900 away. If you lose the remaining $100, get out of the game. More often than not, the easiest way to know that the cards are going against you is to lose the remnants of the original win, see it evaporate from the table. Your message is then very clear—leave.

Always leave a winner. If you can do that, you can't go wrong.

A final note. In sports betting, you must start with a sufficient stake as outlined in the opening section of this chapter. If winning continually, you should increase your bets accordingly. Double them if you've built up your bankroll, and on certain games where you have inside information, bet more heavily.

For example, if you bet an average of three football games a weekend but you find inside information that makes you feel a certain game is a sure thing, then bet your normal three bet total on this game. If this inside information has worked out before, make it five times the normal bet and forget about the other bets. You don't need action; what you need are wins.

And finally, there are players who won't have time for a weekend of gambling but will play only at one session or perhaps two. They might just have a day off and go down to Vegas or Atlantic City or find a poker game somewhere. In casino games, look at your bankroll and divide by 40 and, even better, by 50. That will determine your neutral bet at blackjack and your line bet at craps. If you come to the table with $100, then you're going to make an opening bet in blackjack of $2; and in craps, the same $2 will be your line bet. If you bring $500, then the bets will be in the $10 range.

In poker, use a figure such as 50 times the maximum bet as your needed bankroll. Or, in reverse, divide your bankroll by 50 and that's the biggest bet you should be able to make at a poker game. If you have $100 burning a hole in your pocket, don't get into more than a $1 to $2 game, and better still, play in a $1 maximum game, which will be safer for your kind of bankroll.

If possible, don't depend on one session of play to win money. You should win in the course of several sessions and the longer you play with the information you've gotten in this book, the better your chances of coming out ahead. In the long run, you'll be a winner.

XVI. SELF-CONTROL

If I were to name the one key factor in gambling that makes the difference between winning and losing, it would be self-control. No matter how skillful you are, no matter how much you've studied a game, if you don't have self-control, you're not going to win.

It is my contention that the odds are 2–1 against you whenever you enter a casino. First, you're fighting the house and its edge, and secondly and most important, you're fighting yourself. If you can't control your own feelings, there's no way you're going to win. You've got to have self-control; and while it can't be learned in the same way that you can learn a strategy at a particular gambling game, it still must be mastered for you to be a winner.

To learn the correct moves at a game, such as blackjack, is a study in reason and intellect; to learn self-control, we must move into the realm of feelings. But feelings are just as important as reason, not only in life, but in gambling, and unless you know how your feelings operate and have complete mastery over them, there's no way you're going to end up a winner.

I lived in Las Vegas for a couple of years, at two different points in my life, and I've visited gambling casinos in Europe and the Caribbean, and I've seen literally thousands of gamblers at the tables. Not only have I seen them, which anyone can do, but I made it my business to study them. If you watch a man or woman at a gambling table, after a short while, you know whether or not the person is going to be a winner. It has nothing to do with the number of chips on the table or the game he or she is playing. All you have to do is watch their self-control; or more often, the lack of it.

Simply stated, self-control is the ability to remain in possession of your basic feelings in time of stress. It is also the ability to adhere to a sound strategic plan in the face of adversity and not succumb to the temptations wrought by fear or panic. In real life, it can be a life-saving blessing; in gambling situations it prevents disintegration of the bankroll.

In the course of my professional life, I've taught a great many people how to gamble, and specifically, how to beat games like craps and blackjack. It was most disconcerting to watch them afterwards in a casino, armed with sufficient knowledge to beat the house, losing their shirts because of lack of self-control.

While in Vegas a couple of years ago, I was visited by an independent producer who was in town to discuss one of my novels as a possible film and also to do some gambling. He knew I had written books on the subject, and he asked me to teach him the fine points of blackjack. We spent several hours in the privacy of my apartment, sitting and going over the basic and advanced strategies of 21, including a good counting system and betting method that was undetectable by casino personnel.

After learning the fine points of the game, he was anxious

to play some blackjack, and so we drove to a nearby hotel, and both of us sat at the same table in the casino. I don't like to give advice at a blackjack table, since it immediately waves a red flag in front of floormen and pit bosses, and thus draws heat; but in this case there was little I had to tell Bill, which is what I'll call the producer.

He learned quickly and he was sharp. His life had been spent in Hollywood, among some tough customers, and he could handle the game well. Bill had told me that he had recently had a big disappointment and had missed out on a couple of huge deals, independent productions that would have established him as a top man in Hollywood. He blamed it all on bad luck; but after watching him at the tables for several hours, I could see why he had failed, and it had nothing to do with luck.

We both won some money at the first casino, and Bill was anxious to get into a bigger game; but the one $25 table there was filled, and so we left and went across to another hotel. He found an empty table at this new casino and took out a roll of bills, getting $25 and $100 chips in return. I stood back and watched him play. And Bill had learned well; he was good. He played boldly, without fear, and when the cards were in his favor, he raised his bets with impunity. Within an hour, he was ahead over $2,000, and, after a short setback, rolled it up to $5,000 in winnings within another hour. At this point I suggested that he take a break for lunch. He waved me away, telling me that he wasn't going to give up with this streak going.

"Then put away $4,000 and play out the remaining thousand," I whispered to him. "This streak can't go on forever."

"Why not?" he asked, ordering another drink. It was his fourth scotch and water.

"Why not? Because you have between 0.5 and a 5 percent edge over the house, and that's all you have. You've had a good run. Put away 80 percent of your winnings, and play with the rest. Increase your bets with the $1,000 you'll have on the table. If you hit another good streak, beautiful. But if you lose it, you'll still have a nice win."

"No way," was his response.

"There's plenty of time," I said. "You can play a lot of blackjack these next couple of days. Take a break."

"Ed, please, please," he said, annoyed at my suggestion. I didn't know why he was annoyed, since he had confessed while learning the game from me that he had never won in blackjack before. But there was nothing I could do but stand and watch him play. I wasn't his partner, though I wish I had been for this session, for nothing had gone wrong with any of his moves. He won most of his double downs and practically all his splits were winners.

Instead of putting away the $4,000, he raised his bets to $300 and $400 a hand, and the inevitable happened. The cards turned, as turn they must. The first $1,000 flew away, as if borne by wings. The rest of his winnings took about twenty minutes to disappear. Everything went wrong. Finally, on a $500 bet, he doubled down, putting another $500 on the table, holding an 11 against the dealer's 6. The dealer turned over an ace in the hole for a soft 17 and had to stand. Bill had drawn the case ace on his 11, and lost his $1,000 on that hand alone.

After his winnings were gone, I tapped him on the shoulder. "Come on, get away from this table."

"For Christ's sake, Ed, are you always this kind of nuisance?"

"What?"

"I can't concentrate with you hanging over my shoulder. Leave me alone. Stop badgering me."

He ordered another drink, and I walked away. I didn't have to take that from him, producer or no producer. My intentions had been to save him from himself, not to bother him, but now he was in the grip of defeat and his self-control had flown away along with his money. I left the casino and went into the hotel coffee shop, ordered a sandwich and tea, lingered there for a little while, and then walked back to the casino. Bill was still at the same table.

As I approached, he was removing the last of his bills from his wallet and smoothing them out, then changing them for casino chips. I stood at a discreet distance and watched him play. Another drink was served to him, and despite the intense air-conditioning in the room, he was continually wiping away sweat from his forehead. In a short while, all the cash was gone.

I left the casino. I never heard from Bill while he was in Las Vegas; in fact, I never heard from him again. That ended all talk about movie deals and such things. I realized that the man had a lot of problems, for his lack of self-control had not only ended our business arrangement but also a possible friendship—and of course had wiped him out at the tables.

What causes this kind of behavior? The answer is very complex, but the results are simple. The results are agony and loss and complete change of personality. If you can't take control over yourself, don't gamble till you can.

Even though you can't know all the motivations for your behavioral patterns, you can still set up safeguards to keep your self-control in gambling situations. If you adhere to the following safeguards in any betting situation, you will automatically have control over yourself, no matter what your feelings might be at the moment.

• If you gamble and win, then you must ensure that you will leave the table a winner.

This statement is stressed over and over again in this book, but it can't be repeated enough. If you've won a small amount of money in a game, and the cards or dice are going back and forth in no discernible pattern, get out a winner. For example, if you've started with $500 in a craps game, and after an hour's play, with the dice seesawing, neither hot nor cold, and you're ahead $80, get away from the table. Leave a winner. After an hour, you're probably tired and a break would be welcome, and so why not leave a winner rather than a loser?

If you're winning a great deal at the same craps table, let's say $500, then use our formula for pocketing money, outlined in the chapter on money management. If you're making $10 line and come bets and taking single odds, then each betting cycle will ccst you $60. Allow for two complete rolls, leave $120 on the table, and put away the rest. If you lose the $120, you'll still leave the table with a nice win. And if you continue to win, beautiful.

If you're playing blackjack and are ahead $500, put anywhere between 70 and 80 percent of the win in your pocket as an assured win. If the game has been going on for a long time and you're getting weary, then pocket $400 of the winnings. If you're still fresh, then pocket $350. But make sure that you leave a winner by never touching the money you've put away.

If the producer had followed this formula, at the worst he would have left with $3,500 in winnings, fresh and fit, ready for play that afternoon or the next day. Instead, he crawled out of Vegas like all the other losers, beaten and feeling stupid, angry not only at himself but the whole world.

- Always set a limit on your losses.

Once you've set a loss limit, never deviate and pull more money out of your wallet to play with. *Never.* If you follow only this safeguard, you're assured of self-control. If you divide your bankroll into ten equal parts for a bout of gambling, then, when you've lost one session's limit, get out of the game; no ifs, and, or buts. Don't reach into your pocket for more cash. *The first loss is the cheapest.* Never forget this.

If my friend had followed my advice, he could have been around for another day's play, even after he blew all his winnings. His basic bankroll would still have been intact. If you follow this advice, instead of being wiped out, you will always have another chance to recoup the losses. *Anyone can lose. Everyone must lose at sometime or other,* no matter how skillful or how lucky. But losing doesn't and shouldn't mean total disaster with one crazy binge at a table.

Give yourself ten lives at the gambling table. Lose only one-tenth of your bankroll at any one time. You have nine chances to get it back. The odds are in your favor now. But if you lose half your bankroll at one session, you're in trouble. Even though you have half your money remaining, the seeds of despair have been planted. You won't think correctly; you'll probably do one of two equally dangerous things—either play scared or play like a wild man. Doing either one is putting you on the road to ruin.

- If you are losing, don't chase losses with bigger bets.

To have self-control, you must have a sound method of play, a strategy not only for correct moves but for correct betting. If you deviate either way, you're in deep trouble. When you bring money to the table as your temporary bankroll for that session, that sum of money determines the limits of your betting. If you bring $500 to a blackjack table, your neutral bet can be $10, not $25 or $50.

You're betting $10 because that's all you can afford to bet and maintain your bankroll for the longest possible time, tempered also with the fact that you want to make some real money out of the session, if the cards go your way. If you bet $2 as your neutral bet, you can last a longer time at the table if losing, but you won't be making enough during a winning streak in proportion to your bankroll. And on the other hand, if you bet $25 as your neutral bet, you won't have enough to withstand a temporary setback. Thus you work out a delicate balance, discussed in full in the chapter on money management.

Although there is a strong temptation when losing to make a few big bets and get even fast, that's the worst thing you can do. You're losing because at the moment you're involved in a temporary run of bad luck, and raising your bets at this point isn't going to change your luck or the composition of the cards or the way the dice will bounce. Increased bets are only going to wipe you out that much faster. You must be patient and learn to ride out bad streaks and not yield to temptation by trying to turn the tide with big bets.

When you're in the midst of a losing streak, you know it because of your losses. That's all you know. You can't know when the streak will end. It will end when you start recouping your losses and not before. To use up your bankroll before this happens is foolhardy and dangerous.

I've seen situations where gamblers were wiped out at the craps table by continually raising their bets in a bad losing streak when the dice were cold, and then, five minutes later, as they were nursing a drink and their bruises at a nearby bar, they watched in dismay as the dice turned and got hot at the same table. They knew the dice were hot because of the screams of joy from those still at the table, as numbers and points came up in rapid succession. All they could do was watch and gulp their drinks.

The same thing happens in blackjack, during the course of a season in baseball, in all gambling situations. If you're tapped out, you can't take advantage of winning streaks. *You must ride out losing streaks so that you're still around when the tide turns, otherwise you'll just be around for the losing streaks.*

• Don't do anything that will loosen your hold on your feelings.

Self-control is a fragile thing and has to be held onto carefully. In the frantic world of gambling, with gambling fever rampant, it's easier to go wild or crazy, to throw caution to the winds, to let it all hang out. This is not the place to lose inhibitions, for the consequences are painful and can damage you for a long time.

The easiest way to lose self-control is to loosen up your inhibitions. And an easy way to do that is to drink while gambling. Drugs are another way, but drinking is more tempting, since the casino is going to try and ply you with free drinks. They're giving you the free drinks not because they're altruistic but because they know it will give them bigger profits.

If you want to sip a weak drink while gambling, that's one thing. I often have a sherry or Kahlua and cream or something similar and nurse it for a long time. But you cannot do serious gambling and drink seriously at the same time, without dire consequences. Some of the biggest losers I've ever seen were drunks, and I was sure that they wouldn't have bet in the same insane manner if they were sober and knew what they were doing.

Being drunk while playing for money is stupid. The losing drunk is the most pathetic figure in the casino. Even if you're not drunk, but high or tight, your inhibitions are going to be shaken away, and you might do some very foolish things. And in a game of skill, such as poker or blackjack, you're just asking for trouble, because alcohol is going to erode your skill.

Losers drink and drinkers lose. The winners can't afford to drink. They're too smart to drink while playing for stakes. They know better. The best poker players in the world drink nothing stronger than coffee when they play for unlimited stakes. And they feast off the drunks who fortify themselves with alcohol.

- Finally, don't give up.

When I write "give up," I mean it literally. I've seen players, who, when losing, empty their pockets and do everything possible to lose all their money so they can leave the table.

You can leave the table without doing this. If you've had a bad losing streak, when you get to your loss limit, be gone! Don't wait until you're so tired and depressed that you want to lose everything. At that point, you're flirting with the ultimate loser's philosophy—playing to lose. Play to win. Save your money.

If that terrible losing feeling comes over you, pull yourself together and firmly get up and go. Go anywhere but not to a gambling situation. And then don't gamble for a while till you examine your feelings and know what's happening. If you can't figure out your feelings, get help, either through Gambler's Anonymous or a similar organization or from a private therapist.

When you give up this way, you're not fit to gamble. You're on a bad trip, and you must get off that journey before you wager money again. Anyone can fall into that situation; it's not the end of the world. We all get depressed, and there are times when we want to just give up. All of us have an inner strength that pulls us back to reality, but sometimes it's harder in gambling, when we give up, not our life, but money.

These five safeguards should stand you in good stead. If nothing else, they'll fortify your self-control and make you hold onto your inner strength. Always be aware and refer to these safeguards because the world of gambling is a frantic one, where your feelings are hurtled about in spasms of losing and tension, and unless you stand like a rock, unless you know what you're doing at all times, you'll end up like that vast mob of losers who feed the casino operators with huge profits.

You don't want to make the casino owners rich; you want their money. That's why you're gambling—to win—and self-control is the key to winning.

XVII. GAMBLING TO WIN

If you want to gamble, why not gamble to win? Why not make winning your life-style? It's just as easy to win as to lose, but you must know what you're doing, and you must approach the gambling situation with the right attitude as well as the right strategy.

Have a Positive, Winning State of Mind

Decide that you're going to gamble in order to win money, and that's the only reason you're going to gamble seriously. Just taking this kind of positive, affirmative stance sometimes makes all the difference between winning and losing.

Don't go into a gambling situation thinking of how much you're going to lose and what excuses you'll be giving for your losses. If you think this way, you're doomed before you start.

You can't be on the defensive—you must have a positive frame of mind and an aggressive stance. If on a particular day you can't get into this frame of mind, don't gamble. Hold off until you feel confident again. There may be a lot of reasons you feel defensive and negative, and it might be impossible to fathom them at the time, but your feelings are telling you something, and that message is "don't gamble today."

Set a limit on losses but no limit on wins

In addition to feeling positive about gambling to win, you must set your loss limits and decide that you want to win a lot of money, so much that the casino will be hurting. At the same time, you don't want to become greedy and fight the odds or a bad situation, and the desire to win a lot of money always must be tempered with the fact that you must quit a winner.

A casino owner in Las Vegas once said, "The typical gambler will allow himself to lose far more than he will permit himself to win. This is the biggest edge the house has." Don't be this kind of gambler. Go for all the marbles, but remember, in order to win big, you've got to bet big, and the best way to make large bets is when you're winning, using the casino's money as a wedge and as leverage to hurt the casino.

Study the section on money management to see what bankroll and what individual limits you should set. Using this as a guide, go after the casino or the bookmaker and make him hurt. Make him think of excuses why he lost that day, not the other way around.

To be a winner, you must leave the table a winner

I've made this statement a number of times already, yet I can't repeat it often enough. If you're winning at a table, leave a winner. Leave with most of your winnings. Don't ever put yourself in a position of dropping all of a big win, giving it back to the house. Keep most of it. These winnings add up and then allow you to start play again at another table with the casino's money. When you're playing with their money, everything is easy, and there's no pressure on you. Leave a winner.

Study the section on money management to determine just how much you should set aside of your winnings when you're ahead, and adhere to that formula. It's tried and true and has been worked out under actual gambling and casino situations.

Never reach into your pocket or wallet after setting a loss limit

If you are losing, as you must at times, when you have reached the limit previously set, leave the table. Don't reach in for reserve funds.

Remember, and I repeat this again, *the first loss is the cheapest.* The smaller the loss in proportion to your bankroll, the more chances you have of recouping that loss. The hardest thing to learn is to leave the table, either when you've reached your loss limit, or when you've lost some of your winnings. This ability is what separates the winners from the losers.

Choose a specific area of gambling and stick to it

At the most, involve yourself in two areas of gambling. For instance, you may find that blackjack is your best game, a game that comes easy to you and one you can beat regularly, but you also may find that you can win money betting on pro football games. That's fine, but don't generalize beyond these two areas. Don't take your winnings from blackjack and blow them at baccarat or your winnings from football and blow them on basketball games. This is the age of specialization, and you should become a specialist. Pick the betting areas you can win at, and don't deviate just for the sake of action.

Specialization is of prime importance and must be one of your cornerstone rules of betting. For example, I know successful bettors who wager on college basketball teams but can't make money betting the pro games. And to go even further, I know *really successful and rich* gamblers who bet only on one or two conferences in college basketball. They subscribe to all the college newspapers and home town papers in these conferences and know what's going on through inside contacts. *Knowledge is power in gambling*. I can't repeat this statement often enough.

Some successful gamblers bet on only a few teams in pro football. They know these teams cold and know the circumstances under which the pro line is established. I know a gambler who made a fortune betting against the San Francisco 49ers for a couple of seasons by betting with a San Francisco bookie. The locals loved the team, and yet it was a mediocre and losing team. He could always get a few extra points betting in San Francisco, and if he couldn't get action with the bookie, he got it from individual bettors. They were blinded by allegiance, while he had no allegiance except to winning, and win he did. He decimated the local crowd in the Bay Area for two straight seasons.

There are probably a great many casual gamblers who don't really take advantage of their real interests. Many gamblers love sports and follow a particular team or conference, yet they never put this knowledge to work by betting on what they truly know and feel. Instead, they want action and dissipate their energies, and more importantly, their resources, on games they know nothing about.

I knew a gambler in Vegas who was forever betting games like Harvard–Brown and Colgate–Cornell, though his real love was the Pac 10, because he wanted action and he wanted to be able to get the early results from the eastern part of the country. He didn't know the Ivy League from the ivory tower, and he got buried in the process.

In games like poker, limit your play to a specific game. Find the game that best suits your style, one that you are comfortable with, and that makes money for you. You might find that you prefer draw poker, with its two betting rounds, over a game like seven-card stud, with its five betting rounds. If this is so, and you can make money at the game, stick to draw poker.

And, if you like draw poker, you may find that high draw, with its wider varieties of hands, is more to your style than the slower game of lowball. If this is so, don't play lowball, but stick to high draw. Be the best at that one game, specialize, and you're on your way to winning money from gamblers who will play in any poker game and are mediocre at all of them.

Before you bet real money, make certain that you can win playing the game at home for imaginary money

If you can't win at home, without pressure, without risking real money, don't expect to win from the casino or bookmaker. Most gamblers don't even try to win at home first but wade in with real cash to gambling situations, take a terrible beating, and find themselves without their bankroll in short order. Don't be like them; for they're certain to be losers. Practice at home first, and make sure you can beat the game there before venturing out into the gambling world.

There's a big difference between losing imaginary money betting sports events or casino games at home and losing the same money as real money. For one thing, actual betting with real cash creates all kinds of tensions and problems that don't exist with imaginary bets. Suppose you're betting paper money at home and are down $550 in mind bets in basketball. Your imaginary bankroll was $1,000. You still have $450 in imaginary money left and you're still thinking clearly and don't have to change your strategy.

But if you had really lost that $550 with a bookie, you might be in a daze and might give up a method of winning that is valid because of the pressures of temporary losses.

Many gamblers, particularly those with "systems," go broke quickly because they haven't really tested the systems adequately. They've disregarded huge losing streaks as "freak situations" that wouldn't happen under actual conditions. But it has been my observation that such "freak situations" happen all the time in casinos. *They're the rule, not the exception.* Don't hide your head in the sand. If you can't cut it at home, you're going to be doubly buried at the casino, where the pace is frantic and where the conditions aren't ideally suited to slow, methodical calculations.

In a game like poker, you can't really play at home against imaginary opponents, so it is going to be impossible to have a winning record on paper before you play for actual money. Therefore, you must play the game under actual battle conditions, and the best and easiest way to do this is to play in the smaller games, games in which you don't feel that much pressure. *If you can't beat the small games consistently, don't go into bigger games.* If you can win money in the small games, then enter a game more in line with your bankroll, and see how you do there. Move up to bigger games only when you've beaten the smaller games.

Prepare a strategic plan, and don't deviate from that plan

As you approach the gambling area you have chosen, you

must plan a basic strategy for that particular game, and if that strategy has been tried and proven, you mustn't deviate from it. When choosing a strategy, pick one that will be flexible enough to cover unexpected events.

For example, let's say you're going to play in a seven-card stud game at a Nevada casino. The game is a $3 to $6 one, and you've brought a sufficient bankroll to the game in accordance with proper money management. You've made a careful study of the game and know the correct odds and the right moves for all situations. You've already tested them under actual battle conditions in $1 to $2 games and have won convincingly. You've learned to play an aggressive game and have made other players fear you.

However, in this game, you find that you're playing not only against the usual ragtag of mediocre players but against two drunks as well, who are into every pot and betting as if there's no tomorrow.

Now it's time to alter your strategy. You can go in with weaker hands against these drunks, and you might want to play an even more aggressive game with the first three cards dealt to you, trying to drive out the other players by constant raises so that you can be alone in the pots with the drunks. Deviating from a strong, tight game would be useful here, because it is called for by the presence of the drunks.

When playing other games, such as blackjack and craps, you must approach the game with a definite betting and playing strategy. In blackjack, which is a game of skill, you should not deviate from betting in accordance with card counts; and in craps, you shouldn't make any bet in which the house has an edge of more than 0.8 percent; and you should make only line and come or don't-come bets with odds to keep that edge to a minimum.

When betting sports events, don't be dissuaded by rumors or by other people's bets. If you're waiting on line at a Las Vegas sports book to bet $100 on the Chicago Cubs against the

Phillies, and the man in front of you bets $3,000 on the Phillies, make your $100 bet on the Cubs. Your statistics may be more valid than his money. Stick to your winning methods and use them as your basic strategy, planned and rehearsed before you're actually placing your bets.

Doing this will make you a more intelligent gambler than 95 percent of the people who gamble. Those 95 percent don't know what they'll do most of the time. They stare at the odds or the game, clutching their money in damp hands, knowing they want action, but without any plan to make money. They bet on hunches and change their minds about bets continually. If they win, they don't know why and lose it right back, and if they lose, they expect to lose and feel the situation is normal.

Don't be part of the losing mob. Play to win. Using these basic principles and following the other principles outlined in this book will make you a winner.

INDEX

Edwin Silberstang, currently a resident of San Francisco, has been a member of the New York State Bar, and is a recognized authority on gambling. He is now a full-time writer and senior editor of *Gambling Times* magazine. Silberstang has published five novels, and his non-fiction books include *Playboy's Book of Games, Las Vegas: An Insider's Guide,* and *Winning Poker Strategy,* among others.